Great Masters

Acknowledgments
The publishers would like to thank the museums for reproduction permission and in particular the **BRIDGEMAN ART LIBRARY** for their help in supplying the illustrations for the book.
Albertina Graphic Collection, Vienna: Castle Court (Innsbruck); Turkish Horseman; Nuremburg Woman Dressed for Church; Young Hare; Great Piece of Turf; Christ on the Cross; Arion; Hands.
Alte Pinakotek, Munich: Self-Portrait; The Four Apostles (Detail) St John and St Peter; The Four Apostles (Detail) St Mark and St Paul.
British Museum, London: The Castle of Trent; Pine Tree; Pond in a Wood; Three Turkish Figures; Emblematic Design with a Crane; Apostle; Fountain; House on an Island in a Pond.
Burghley House, Stamford: St Eustache.
Christie's, London: Bearing of the Cross; Wing of a Blue Roller; The Rhinoceros.
Galleria degli Uffizi, Florence: Portrait of Dürer's Father; Self-Portrait; St Philip.
Guildhall Library, Corporation of London: Melancholy I.
Kunsthistorisches Museum, Vienna: Virgin Suckling Child; Portrait of a Venetian Girl; Adoration of the Trinity; Flood (Dream Vision).
Louvre, Paris: Self-Portrait with Eryngium Flower.
Prado, Madrid: Adam; Eve; Portrait of a Gentleman.
Private collection: The Four Horsemen of the Apocalypse; The Whore of Babylon -The Apocalypse.

Published by Park Lane
An imprint of Grange Books PLC
The Grange
Grange Yard
London SE1 3AG

This edition published 1994

ISBN 1 85627 517 5

Albrecht Dürer

PARK
LANE

His Works

Albrecht Dürer
His Life and Works

Although Albrecht Dürer's name is intimately linked to Nuremberg, where he was born and lived, in all of German cultural history only Bach and Goethe are of comparable stature. In the late fifteenth century, Nuremberg was one of the busiest, most liberal and cultured of German cities. There was, however, no equivalent artistic ferment to match the humanistic and scientific development.

Art remained firmly anchored to the Gothic style and to the works through which many artists had carried this style to a formal perfection. Although in Italy the Renaissance sprang almost spontaneously from past experiences, in Germany it was greeted with little conviction. This was not due to any basic prejudice, but rather to an incapacity to thoroughly absorb new concepts, which would have required not only a "rebirth" in terms of art, but also a total commitment to radical social transformation to which medieval Germany was not predisposed.

Albrecht Dürer of Nuremberg, however, consciously forced himself to attempt the marriage between the centuries-old pictorial and expressive traditions to which he was tied and the new influences filtering north from Italy. These concepts not only encouraged a new interest in humanistic and classical art, which already existed in Germany, but also required a profound renewal of culture and thought, involving both taste and means of expression. Thus, as a child of a contradictory era and culture, Dürer found himself obliged, both as poet and craftsman, to resolve the conflicting influences that inspired him. It was this that made him both a modern artist and an innovator.

If it was Dürer's thirst for knowledge that made him travel south to discover new compositional concepts, then it was German tradition that allowed him to express the minute formal refinement of the Gothic artist. Dürer's greatness lies in his capacity to find a synthesis between these influences, and if he succeeded in this difficult task it is because the conscious choices he made were always supported by an astonishing technical mastery of the medium of expression.

Albrecht Dürer was born in Nuremberg in 1471. He was the son of a Hungarian goldsmith who had arrived in the city sixteen years before. In his memoirs, written when he was about fifty-three years old, Dürer recalls his father's workshop where he first demonstrated his extraordinary gift for drawing. At that time the working of gold required great artistic mastery because the goldsmith had to engrave elaborate decorations and figures on jewelry.

In 1486, the young Dürer entered the workshop of Michael Wolgemut as an apprentice. He remained there for three years. By 1484, however, he had completed his first important work, the *Self-Portrait*, a silverpoint drawing in the Dutch style. It was while working with Wolgemut that Dürer's interest in reproductive illustration was born, and this later stimulated him to make engraving a fundamental part of his work.

His earliest surviving signed work, *Portrait of Dürer's Father*, dates from the end of this apprenticeship. Although this piece is characteristic of the Flemish tradition, it already shows a markedly personal vigor and graphic tension. In 1490, Dürer journeyed across the Rhineland, Alsace, and Holland and encountered the work of Hausbuchmeister, a miniaturist and wood-engraver, and admired the graphics of Martin Schongauer. This was a truly formative journey and, like those he would later make to Italy, was decisive in the creation of his individual style.

From 1491 to 1493, Dürer's work was rich and varied. In his *Holy Family* drawings, there is astonishingly vibrant movement reminiscent of Leonardo da Vinci, even though Dürer had probably not yet come into contact with the works of the great Italian artist. There then followed the famous *Self-Portrait with Eryngium Flower*, a painting distinguished by the softness of touch and color, distributed in cold bands of greens, olives, and pinks. In those same years he illustrated the comedies of Terence and other literary works with wood-engravings and completed various drawings based on the sculpture of Nicola Gerhaert from Leida. Even in these early works it seems possible to detect Dürer's concept of figurative art as an instrument of free creation. His output mainly stresses the importance of the human figure, his own included.

In 1494 he completed both free and faithful copies of works by Pollaiuolo and Mantegna and his interest in animalism and the world of chivalry seemed to decline. Between 1494 and 1495 Dürer made his first journey to Italy, where he became more intellectually aware of the problems he had already encountered. Contact with the complex artistic situation in Italy, dominated by such artists as Carpaccio and Mantegna, led him to reflect on the limitations of Nuremberg, where the problems of reinterpreting the classical form using new spatial concepts were yet to be confronted. Although the lessons learned in Italy would prove decisive for the young Dürer, in such works as the studies for *The Rape of the Sabine Women* and *Nude Seen from Behind* a certain reluctance to accept these valuable but partially alien influences can still be perceived. Dürer found himself caught between the different cultures of northern Europe and Italy in a period of great social change, and, as a result, his whole career was characterized by the tension this created.

Thus, in such works as *St. Anthony* and *St.Sebastian*, two sides of the altar in Dresden, Dürer seems to have momentarily set aside what he had learned in Italy. The Italian influence is again visible in such works as *Portrait of Frederic the Wise*, where there is evident contrast between the light, uniform background and the dark cloth with golden ornamentation. *Self-Portrait with Gloves*, 1498, is even closer to the Italian masters, not only for the range of line development, but also because the painter depicts himself as artist and gentleman to affirm the dignity of painting as a liberal art. The fifteen *Apocalypse* wood-engravings are also dated 1498. These are the masterpieces not only of Dürer's work but of all German wood-engraving, which was then renowned throughout Europe. The most striking aspect of this series is a clearly perceived stylistic passage from the first plates, in Gothic composition, to the later plates in which spatial relationships are much more measured, in the manner of Mantegna. This was done to achieve a dramatization that parallels events in the book, the monumentality increasing as one plate follows another. *The Apocalypse* may indeed mark the birth of modern illustration.

The year 1499 brought the superb portraits of the members of the Tucher family. Portrait work allowed Dürer to continue his search for a meeting point between Flemish and Italian traditions; the results of this are both highly original and of great quality. The Tucher family, for example, appears in the foreground with a brocaded background, but the lateral opening of the landscape breaks with Northern tradition and is reminiscent of Bellini. The same year Dürer also completed the important *Self-Portrait with Fur*, where his poetic aspiration is evident. The figure of Dürer is here identified with that of Christ. Having glorified the artist as a gentleman, Dürer now brings him closer to God. the inspiration of all art. The artist is thus ennobled in both a human and a religious sense. This work is also a convincing exaltation of man in his own right; it should not be forgotten that Europe was on the brink of the Lutheran revolution. Leaving aside the painting's ideological content, technically Dürer appears to be developing his study of the Italian masters. The influence of Piero della Francesca, in particular, is visible in the careful study of the human proportions, even if the meticulously planned composition remains concealed beneath an extraordinarily spontaneous appearance.

In these very years in which Dürer achieved great artistic maturity and firmly established himself, he became even more strongly aware of his own limitations and those of the creative potential of the artist. These were not personal limitations, but those of every human being animated by divine power. His writings of the time reflect his concern for the "primary reasons" of things, and he analyzed the specific while never forgoing immersion in what he described as the "universal breath." His interest in literature and philosophy was not surprising. As a result of his close contact with his old friend the German humanist Willibald Pirckheimer and his learned circle, Dürer had become an art theorist and in the two centuries that followed, his scientific works, translated into Latin, were to be as famous as his art.

In the early years of the sixteenth century Dürer used the burin technique for the first time, and all his engravings in this period, including *St. Eustache* and *The Great Fortune*, were created in a climate of intense meditation. These were years of feverish work. With the help of capable colleagues Dürer dedicated himself to continuous experimentation, producing, among other things, *Hercules Killing the Stymphalian Birds*. Although strongly reminiscent of the prints of Pollaiuolo, this work actually offers a Northern reinterpretation of vitalism to the Italian

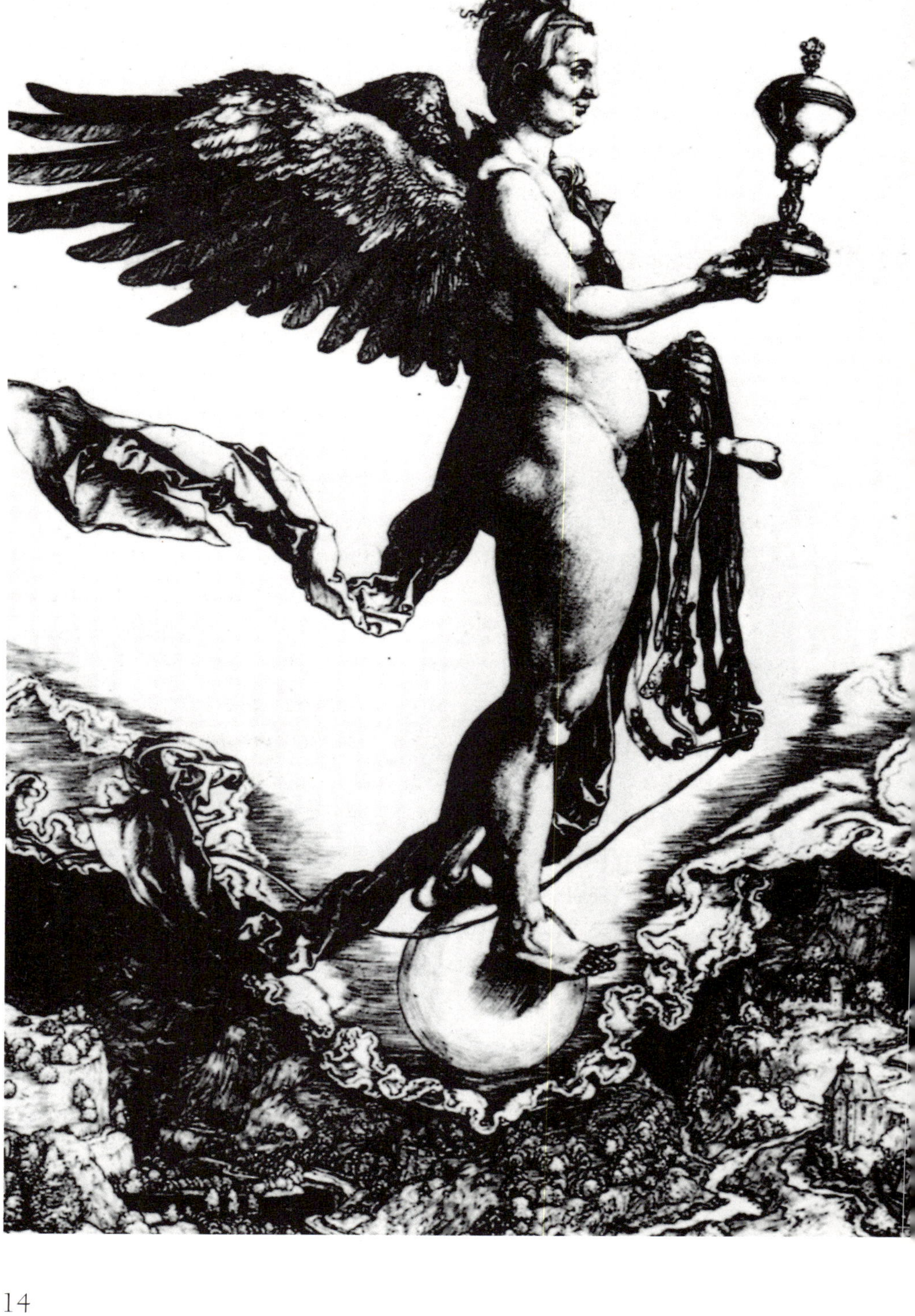

Nemesis
(The Great Fortune
(Detail)

master. *Lament for Christ Dead* was also completed around 1500. This commissioned work is clearly close to the Italian Renaissance, particularly when it is compared with other Dürer works on the same theme. It is a masterly reworking of a theme that was also common to the Flemish artists, but Dürer introduces his own unique voice in the disposition of the figures and their relationship to the background.

Just as there was always a mixture of Northern spirit and Italian Renaissance influences in his art, Dürer's everyday existence was also profoundly split between the public and the private. The constant enmity that divided his wife, Agnes, and his dear friend Pirckheimer was symbolic of this. He had married Agnes Frey in 1491 immediately after he returned from his first journey abroad. Biographers agree that their relationship deteriorated rapidly, and in his writings Dürer gives the same impression by making jocular and fairly caustic references to his wife on a number of occasions. It is certain, however, that Agnes always hated Pirckheimer and the feeling was reciprocated. Dürer's rich and noble friend, to whom he had been close since early childhood, typified the kind of cultured, carefree, Renaissance character so foreign to her medieval "virtue." Although Willibald and his friends presented no threat whatsoever to the unity of her family, Agnes undoubtedly hated him because he embodied that creative, humanistic spirit capable of transforming the simple craftsman she believed she had married into an artist in the modern sense, a technical and spiritual investigator completely dedicated to his own mission. Agnes was certainly not mistaken in regarding Pirckheimer as an example of Renaissance man: this robust and enormously vital person was one of the most important figures in the humanist movement, and his influence on Dürer was certainly considerable. If it had not been for this man of letters and of arms, diplomat and administrator, lover of art and good living, Dürer's relationship with Italian humanism and all that it could represent for a German artist would have been very different. Their friend-

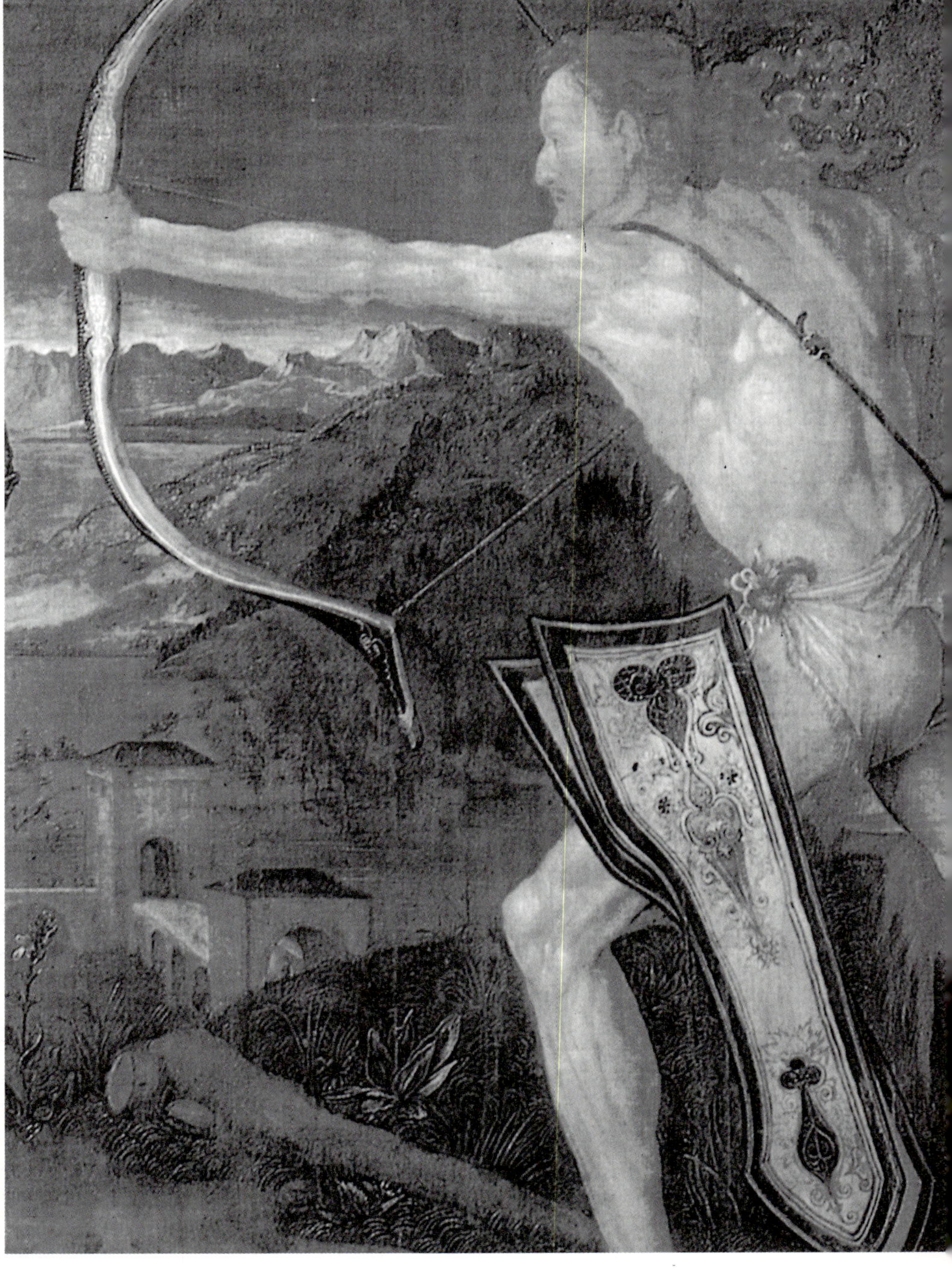

Hercules Killing the Stymphalian Birds (Detail)

ship was cemented by a capacity to mutually improve each other and by a communion of interests that united them throughout their lives.

In 1503 Dürer completed *Virgin Suckling Child*, in which the image stands out against a compact background, while an almost *Mona Lisa* smile plays across the face of the Virgin. There is none of the proportional tension characteristic of the works in which the medieval artist confronted the problems of spatial representation. The following year, in two engravings, *The Nativity* and *Original Sin*, Dürer attempted for the last time the type of experiment that owed much to Bellini and Piero della Francesca in that it concerned forms of absolute theorization. In succeeding works the artist's interest in analytical representation of natural phenomena became evident. *Great Piece of Turf*, 1503, already shows signs of this new influence, where the identification of the most minute particulars and the "aesthetic sublimation of a scientific interest" once again are reminders of Leonardo, whose drawings were certainly known to the German artist. Dürer was now no longer trying simply to solve the problem of perspective but was examining every kind of human expression, even in its most hidden emotional manifestations.

Although the engravings were still concerned with studies of perspective and proportion, his pictorial work now led to a wide range of results, without precluding a respect for Northern tradition. Characteristic of this period is the triptych consisting of *The Adoration of the Shepherds*, and the two lateral wings depicting St. George and St. Eustache. While a Flemish and Dutch spirit is noticeable in this work, it also shows Italian influences personally reinterpreted by Dürer. In 1504 he also completed *The Adoration of the Magi*, a work pervaded by a tender, uniform beauty, once again reminiscent of Leonardo, particularly in the group of horsemen and in one of the wise men.

Germany during this period was struck by a series of epidemics, culminating in the plague of 1505, which motivated Dürer to make his second journey to Italy. The elector of

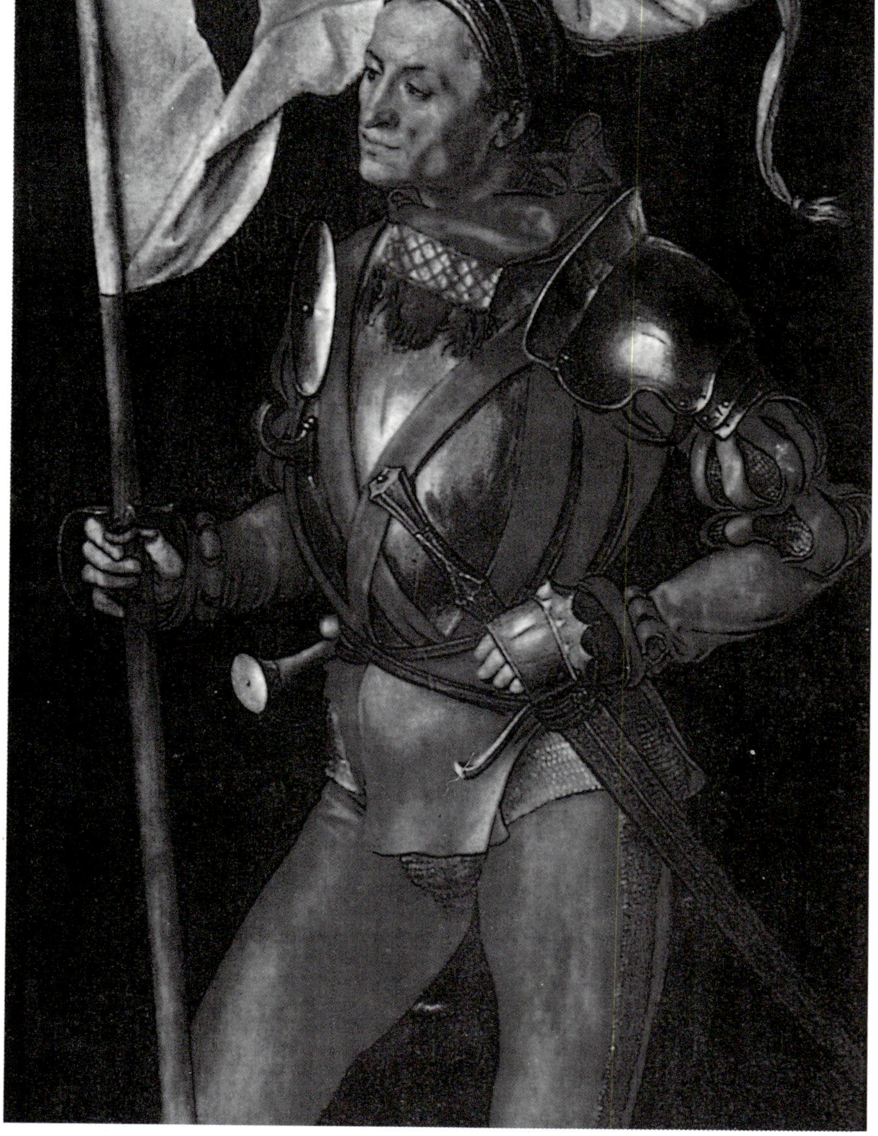

St Eustache
(Detail)

Saxony, Frederic the Wise, had already commissioned *The Story of Job*, a single work that in later years was divided into two fragments, *Job and His Wife* and *The Two Musicians*. By commissioning this painting, Frederic was trying to protect himself from the plague, since Job was venerated as a healer. Certain critics, perhaps overimaginatively, claim to find an autobiographical element in the painting. If one of the two musicians does represent Dürer, it may be deduced that he identified himself, on the one hand, with the patient Job, persecuted by the Agnes of the moment, and, on the other, with the musician, beautiful, different, and proud, above banal family quarrels.

It was not just the plague that drove Dürer once again to Italy. He was also motivated by his observations about the results he had already achieved and by his insatiable spirit of experimentation. Thus, he suddenly abandoned the intense wood-engraving work he was engaged in at the time, an example of which is the famous *Green Passion* cycle. Dürer arrived in Venice in 1505, no longer merely a young man eager to learn, but a famous and established artist.

Fought over and spoiled by Venetian society, he was able to dedicate himself to the purchase of works of art, including oriental art, and books from the renowned printers of the Republic of San Marco. He was also able to spend much time, as he himself wrote to Pirckheimer, with "masters of ingenuity . . . experts in painting and many other noble minds." He came into contact with the small but well-established colony of German merchants and was commissioned by them to paint *The Feast of the Rosary*, one of his most imposing works. Unfortunately, this has survived in such a poor state of conservation, and has been so badly restored, that its importance and beauty can only be imagined. The work is an altarpiece depicting an enthroned Madonna, on one side of whom stands the clergy, including the pope, and on the other, the emperor and nobles. Some people detected a faintly antipapal tone in this painting, since the cult of the rosary symbolized unity around both the church and

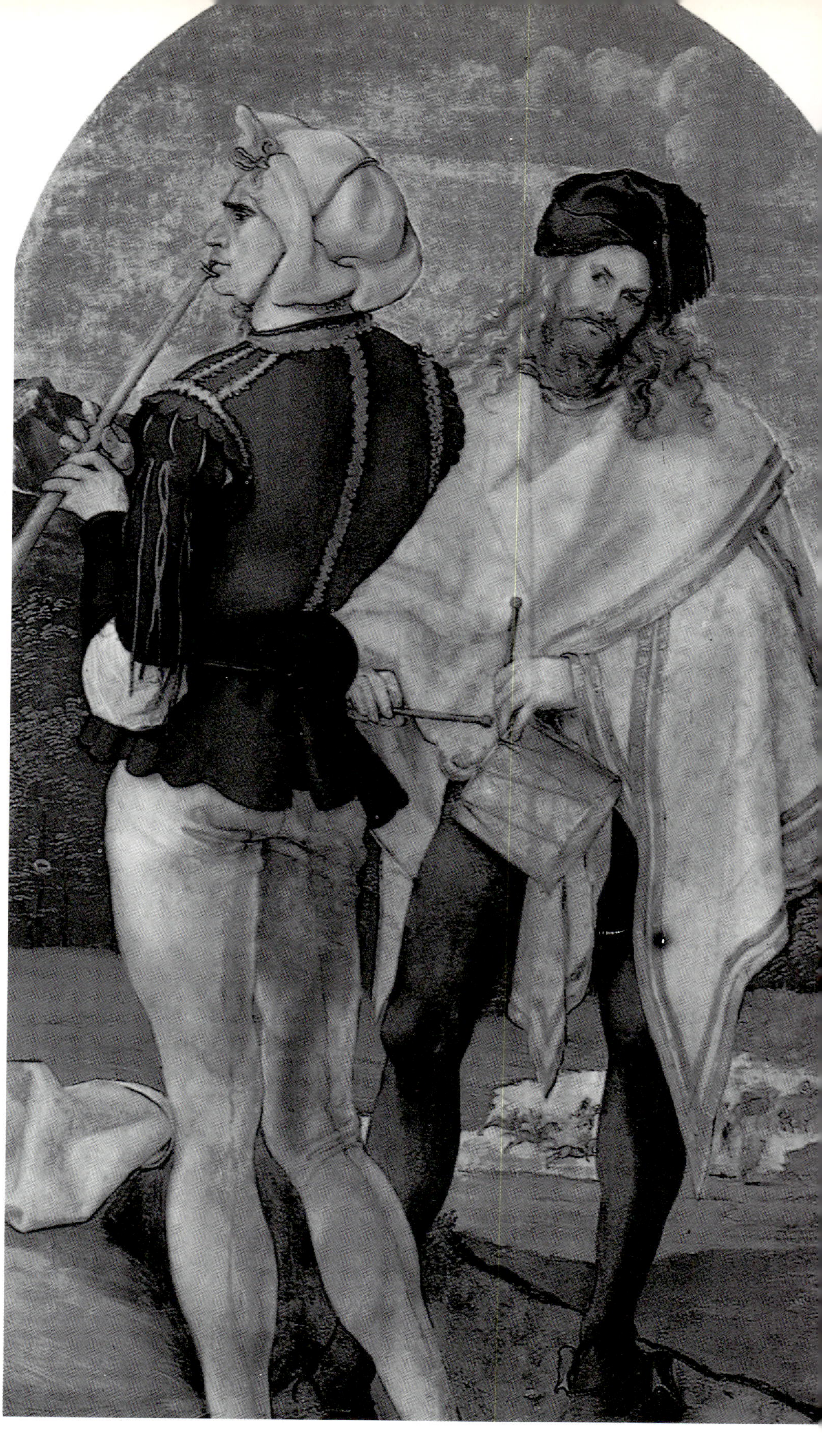

Two Musicians
(Detail)

temporal power, and the images of emperor and pope are both given the same importance.

In Venice, Dürer also painted *The Madonna of the Siskin*, similar to *The Feast of the Rosary* in its representation of perspective and its use of color. In both these works the splendor of the colors is of staggering quality. Almost as a challenge to the new generation of painters who tended to consider him primarily an engraver, in his use of color Dürer proudly places himself alongside the most gifted of them, including Giorgione, who was much admired in Venice at that time.

Christ Among the Scholars also belongs to this Venetian period. Dürer himself described this as "a work the like of which I have never done before." It owes some aspects to certain conceptions of Hieronymus Bosch, but there are also echoes of Leonardo, above all in the figure of the twelve-year-old Christ. This is a work of great significance, for here Dürer seems to set aside the quest for the clear and distinct representation of space, which had characterized his work after his first journey to Italy, to dedicate himself completely to the pungent realism of the image and intense observation of physiognomy. The same is true of *Greed*, where the physicality of the figure is so immediate as to be almost offensive. In this way Dürer contributed to Venetian culture, with a new approach to realistic representation and not merely a concern for space and proportions. It is also worth considering *Portrait of a Venetian Girl*, painted early in his stay in Venice, a portrait notable for its sweetness through which the artist's admiration for the beautiful model shines.

The diversions of the city and his mainly pictorial work in Venice caused Dürer to set aside his engraving for a time, but he never forgot the main reason for his journey to Italy: the search for precise theories as a basis for his art. Typical of this was his search for almost magical formulas to enable him to master "the secret of proportion." This quest took him to Bologna, to meet Luca Pacioli, a friend of Leonardo's, and demonstrates again the

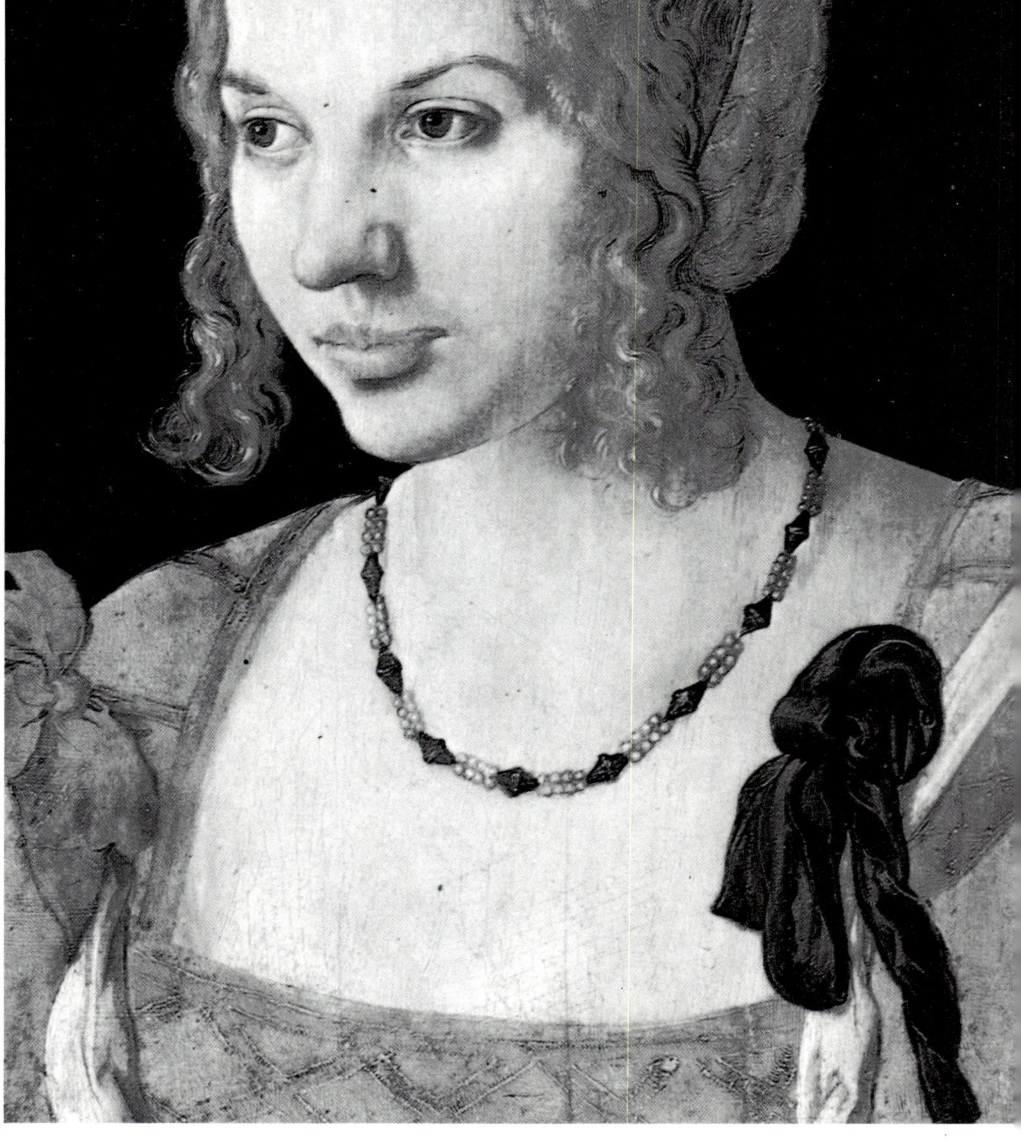

Portrait of a Venetian Girl (Detail)

way Dürer's insatiable thirst for knowledge found fertile ground in Italy. He also appreciated the high regard in which artists were held in Italy: "Here I am a gentlemen," he wrote to Pirckheimer from Venice. "At home I am a parasite."

It was, therefore, with great regret that Dürer decided to return to Nuremberg in 1507, but the importance of his stay in Italy would be evident in his later works. It marked the beginning of what was perhaps the most important period in his career, and it lasted for seven years. He had completely assimilated, and in some cases improved upon, the dictates of the Renaissance, and his solution to the problems of proportion was also noticeably different. Proof of this are the twin paintings *Adam* and *Eve*, which were the first life-sized nudes in German painting. If they are typical of the Renaissance in their quest for ideal human beauty, in a certain sense they go beyond it in their clear violation of the laws of proportion (the figures appear decidedly lengthened) and for their insistence on the grace of the man and the woman. There are those who see the early themes of Mannerism in this (Lukas Cranach the Elder, among others, would later refer to the work), but, in reality, it is difficult to place these two nudes in a precise category. In 1508 Dürer completed *The Martyrdom of the Ten Thousand*, where he created not an architectonically supported spatial structure, but, by progressively reducing the dimensions of the objects depicted the farther they were from the observer, he achieved a three-dimensional representation.

The culmination, however, of this work is to be found in *The Adoration of the Trinity*, known as the Landauer Polyptych after the man who commissioned it. Although dated 1511, this painting is the fruit of numerous previous studies. According to most critics the painting must be seen in context, since the frame constitutes "the gate" of celestial vision. The work is based on an impressively scrupulous study of the rules of perspective, but the most surprising pictorial effect lies in the division of the polyptych into two levels in which there is absolutely nothing

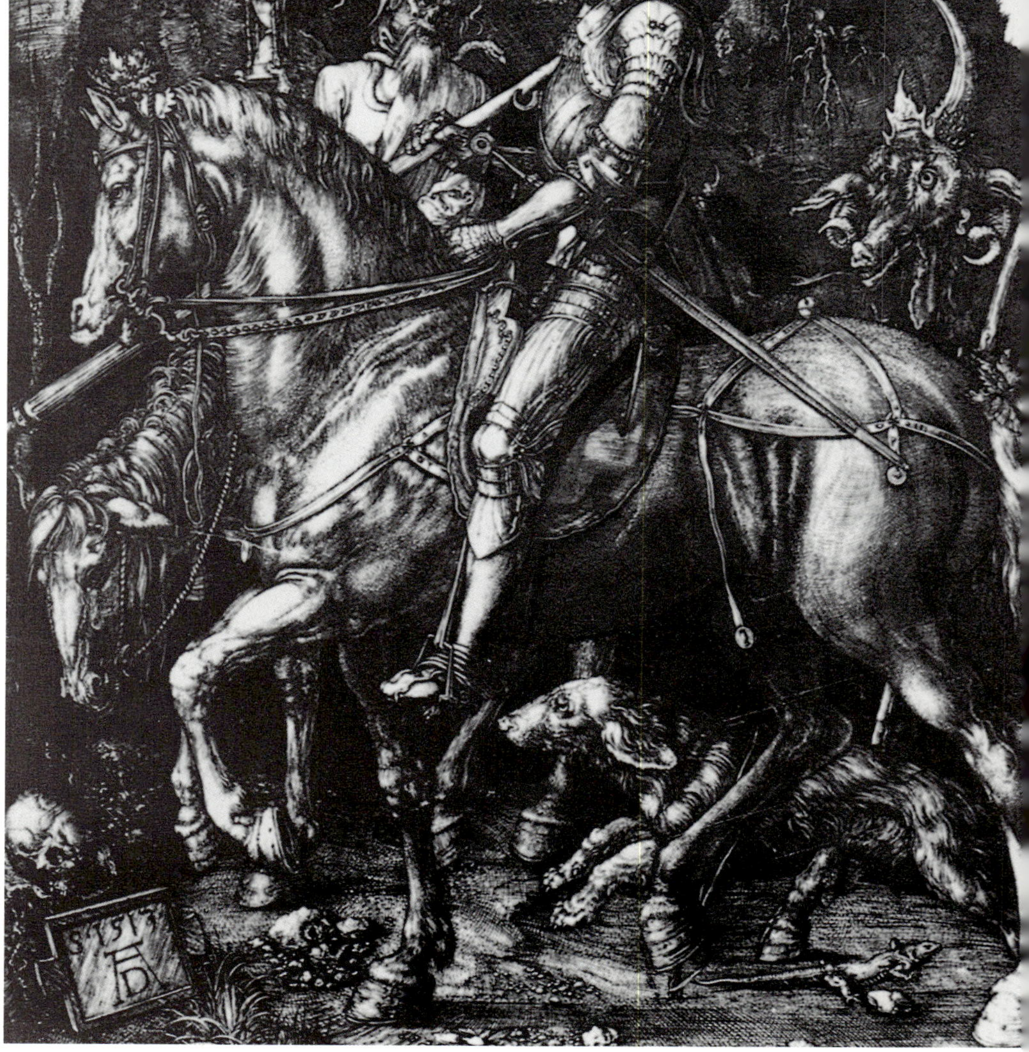

The Knight, Death, and the Devil (Detail)

earthly, only "visions of reality among the clouds," following canons very different even from those of the Renaissance.

After this painting, which in many aspects represents the apex of his pictorial achievement, Dürer dedicated himself once more to engraving, bringing to bear all he had learned in his work with the brush. His studies in perspective are thus applied to the last plates of *The Life of Mary*, 1510, characterized by a new monumentality. The engravings that complete *The Great Passion* and the frontispiece of *The Apocalypse* show evidence of a new style, not only from the point of view of perspective, but also with the introduction of a "medium graphic tone," corresponding to the chiaroscuro of painting and permitting highly refined effects. The year 1511 brought the engravings of *The Little Passion*, which Dürer had begun some time before, and he also worked on engravings for *The Passion*, which were not published until 1513.

Dürer's intentionally "archaic" works, with completely conventional spatial plans, such as *The Emperor Charlemagne* and *The Emperor Sigismund*, 1512-1513, stylistically seem to obliterate years of investigation and experimentation. This temporary "crisis" was overcome in the three great engravings of 1513-1514: *The Knight, Death and the Devil*, *St Jerome in His Studio*, and *Melancholy I*. The first of these is a development of his youthful *St. Eusebio*, but it is now the allegorical theme that dominates the exaltation of the landscape. The heroic character of the whole piece is evident throughout, and an exceptional realism accompanies the unrestrained visionary qualities. The knight's lance confers a diagonal expansion to the scene, and the figures seem to leap into the foreground. There is the same marvelous coordination in the representation of *St. Gerome*, where every form respects precise volume requirements and the line of the burin itself reinforces the principal directional lines of the work and contributes to the representation of space. *The Knight* can be interpreted as a symbol of battle, and complementary to the contemplative existence of *St Jerome* (with the same body of religious views permeating both); *Melancholy I* is much more difficult from the allegorical point of view. It can be interpreted as representing the restless human quest and thus the condition of the artist. Even if it is not possible to affirm that Dürer, in this third engraving, was referring to the melancholy plight of the artist who lacks sufficient faith, undoubtedly he himself could easily have identified with such a situation.

After these three major engravings, Dürer's work assumed rather peculiar characteristics. He renewed his interest almost exclusively in craftwork, involving the participation of many helpers, to complete the important commissions of Maximillian I. From 1515 onward, Dürer received a fixed annual sum of one hundred florins from the emperor: this substantial sum was not always regularly paid, since the emperor's ambitions often exceeded his financial capacity. A cultured humanist and a disorderly but passionate scholar of various disciplines, Maximillian had already contacted Dürer in 1512 for the execution of drawings, plans, and prints. The most grandiose project on which Dürer worked for Maximillian was the *Triumphal Arch*, a gigantic engraving measuring three by three and a half meters. One hundred and ninety-two blocks of wood were needed to print the single sheet of which it was composed. Although Dürer was head draftsman, he does not seem to have been very involved in a project that is mainly the product of the workshop. Of much greater value and exceptional graphic resonance are his drawings for Maximillian's *Book of Prayer*, 1515.

While Dürer continued studying the fundamentals of art, which would later constitute his tracts on measurement and proportion, he once again showed his interest in painting. In *St Philip* and *St James the Apostle* there is a clear search for realism that highlights the most minute particulars of the figures, conferring on them a strong dramatic power that is underlined by the projection of the saints ' heads toward the observer. Even more significant in this sense is the *Portrait of Michael Wolgemut*, 1516, which is of such power as to surpass

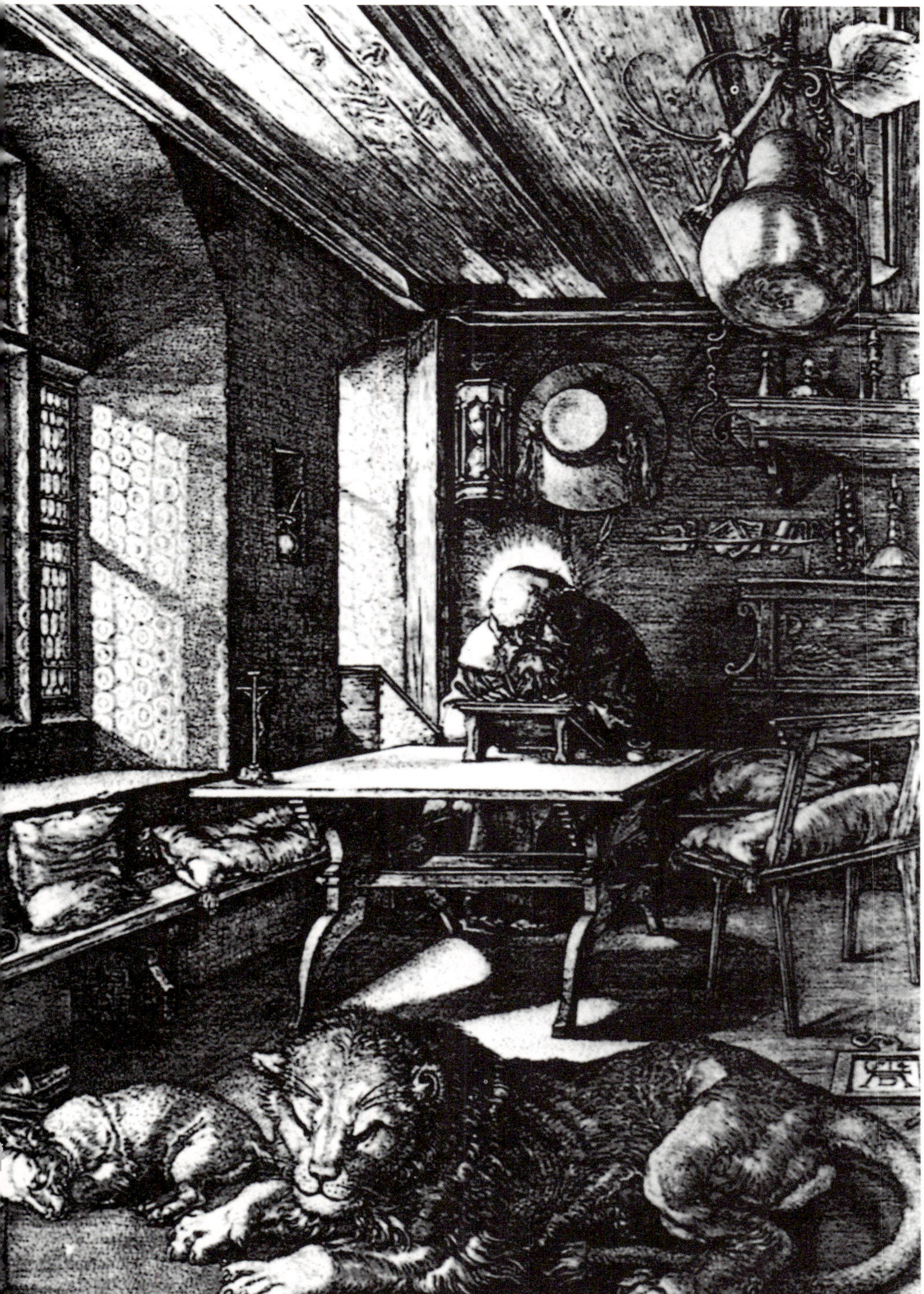

St Jerome
in His Study

the already superb results achieved in the famous *Madonna of the Carnation* of the same year. Deeper sentimental participation, which detracts nothing from theoretical research, is apparent in the image of *St. Anna with the Virgin Child*, 1519.

The new emperor, Charles V, continued Dürer's pension, and this permitted him to make a lengthy journey to the most important Flemish and Dutch cities. In his later years there is a noticeable and substantial stability in the graphic style, less rich in poetry than his earlier periods, but there are still changes in his painting. The two works depicting boys' heads, 1520 and 1521, constitute an advance in terms of realistic results.

The last part of Dürer's life was dedicated to the editing of his writings and he did not produce many paintings. Among these, the two that he donated to the city of Nuremberg are of great importance. These are entitled *The Four Apostles* (*St John the Evangelist and St Peter* and *St Mark and St Paul*) and were probably conceived as the two wings of a tryptich. The symbolic significance of the work is not clear today, but it underlies the entire creation. The controversial implications of the representation are rendered explicit by the inscriptions that refer to the religious situation in the city. Nuremberg had officially adhered to the Reformation only the year before, and Dürer himself had always been interested in Luther and wanted to meet him (he died without realizing this desire). From the point of view of composition, there is formidable tension in the two works, and the monumental nature of the apostles' heads does not detract from a subtle psychological investigation.

Dürer's third theoretical book, on proportion, was published in a double edition, in both German and Latin, in 1528. He died in the April of the same year. He was buried in the churchyard of St. John in Nuremberg, where a large stone marks his grave.

Albrecht Dürer was the first German artist to become internationally famous in his own lifetime. While he was still working in Nuremberg, people abroad were seeking, imitating, and even forging his work. His name was known and respected by publishers, artists, and humanists from Amsterdam to Venice. An enormous amount of work, most of which has fortunately survived, testifies to his abilities.

Painter and engraver, scholar of artistic theory, mathematician, builder, and writer capable of reforming German prose, Dürer was the only man of art of this era in Germany who, in achievements of moral and creative status and variety of activity, can be justifiably compared to the great Italian artists who were his contemporaries. The succession of profound doubts and certainties that colored his entire creative life, and his endless reflection on his art, render Dürer a man of culture who was extraordinarily similar to the modern artist.

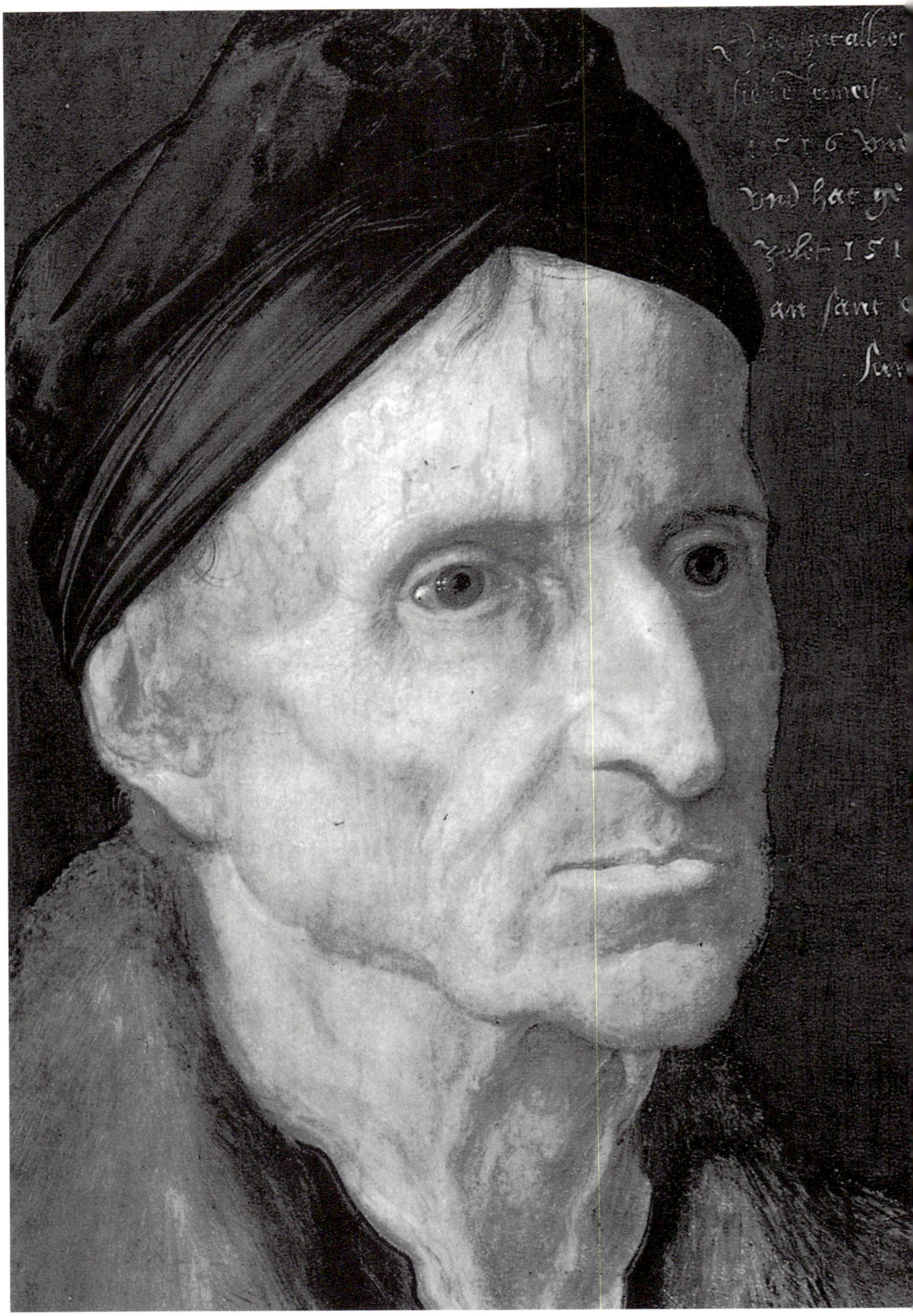

Portrait of
Michael Wolgemut
(Detail)

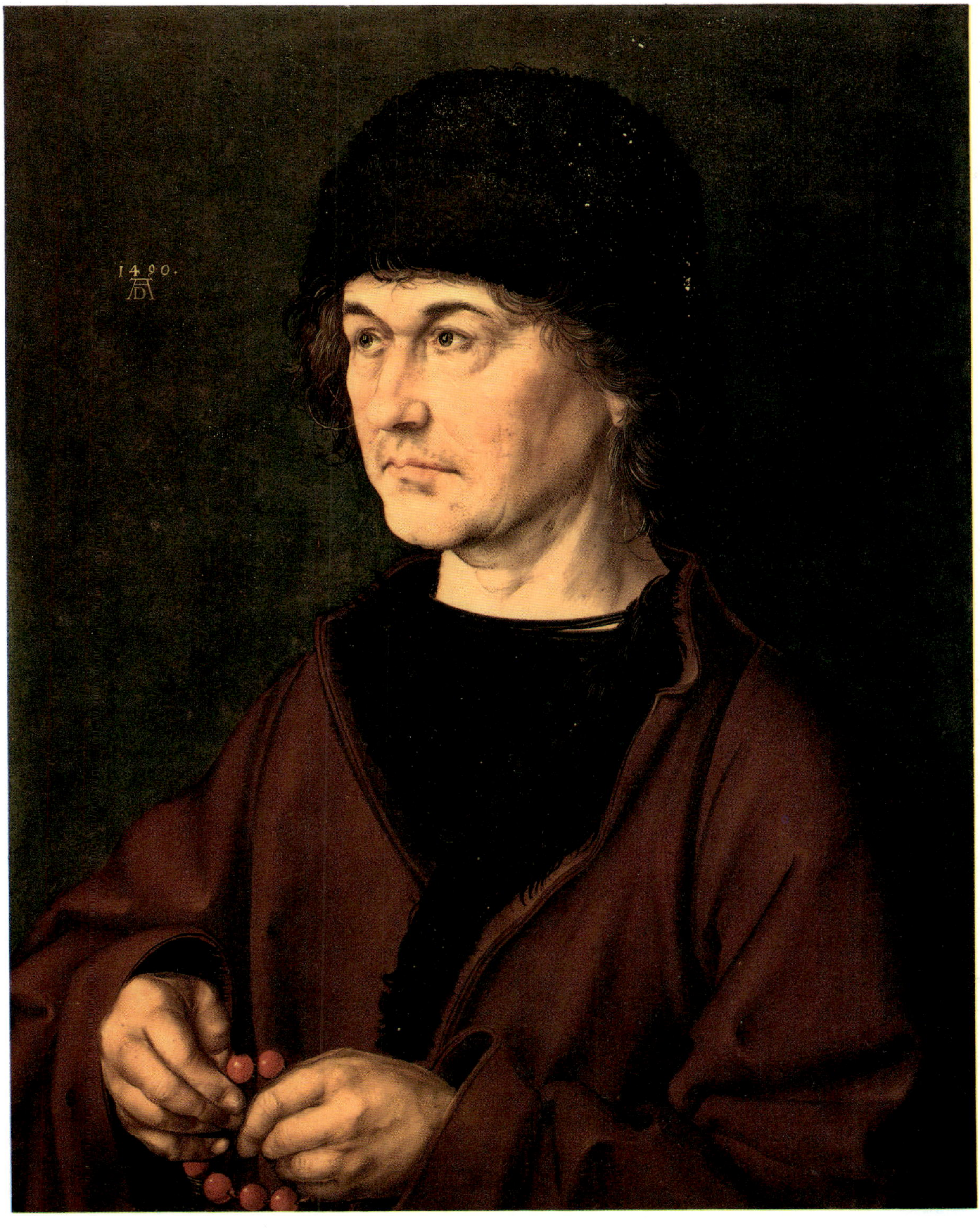

Portrait of Dürer's Father

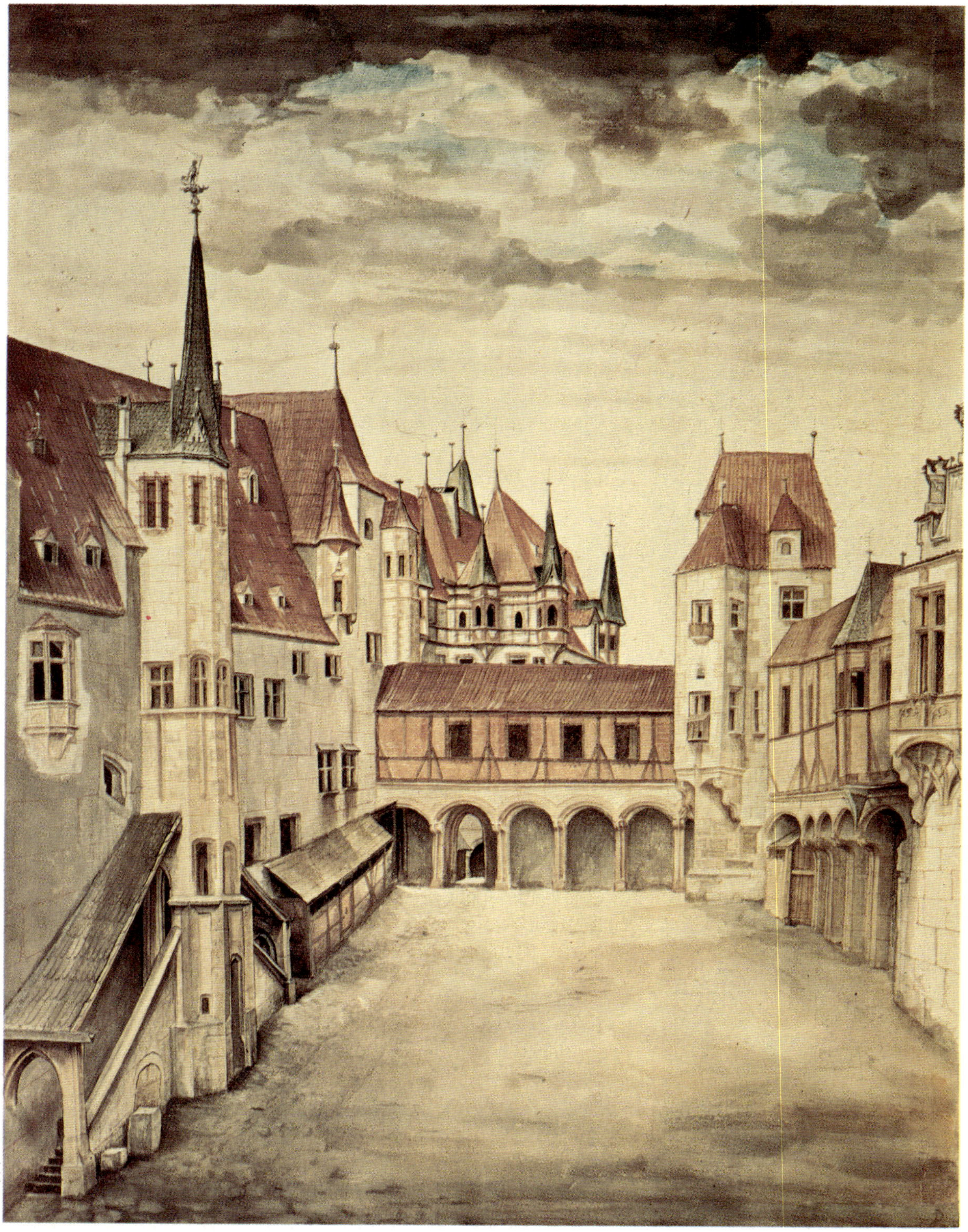

Castle Court (Innsbruck)

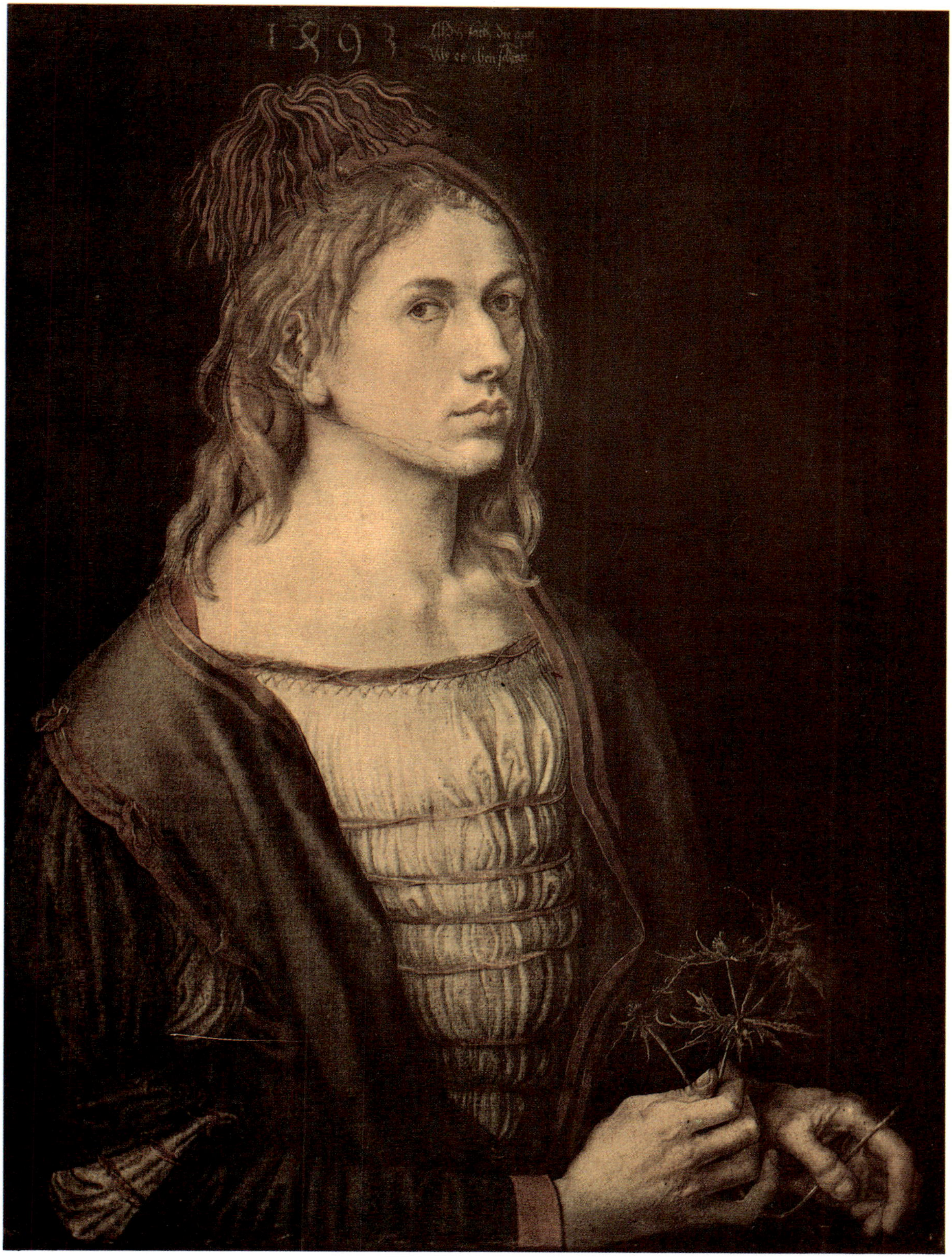

Self-Portrait with Eryngium Flower

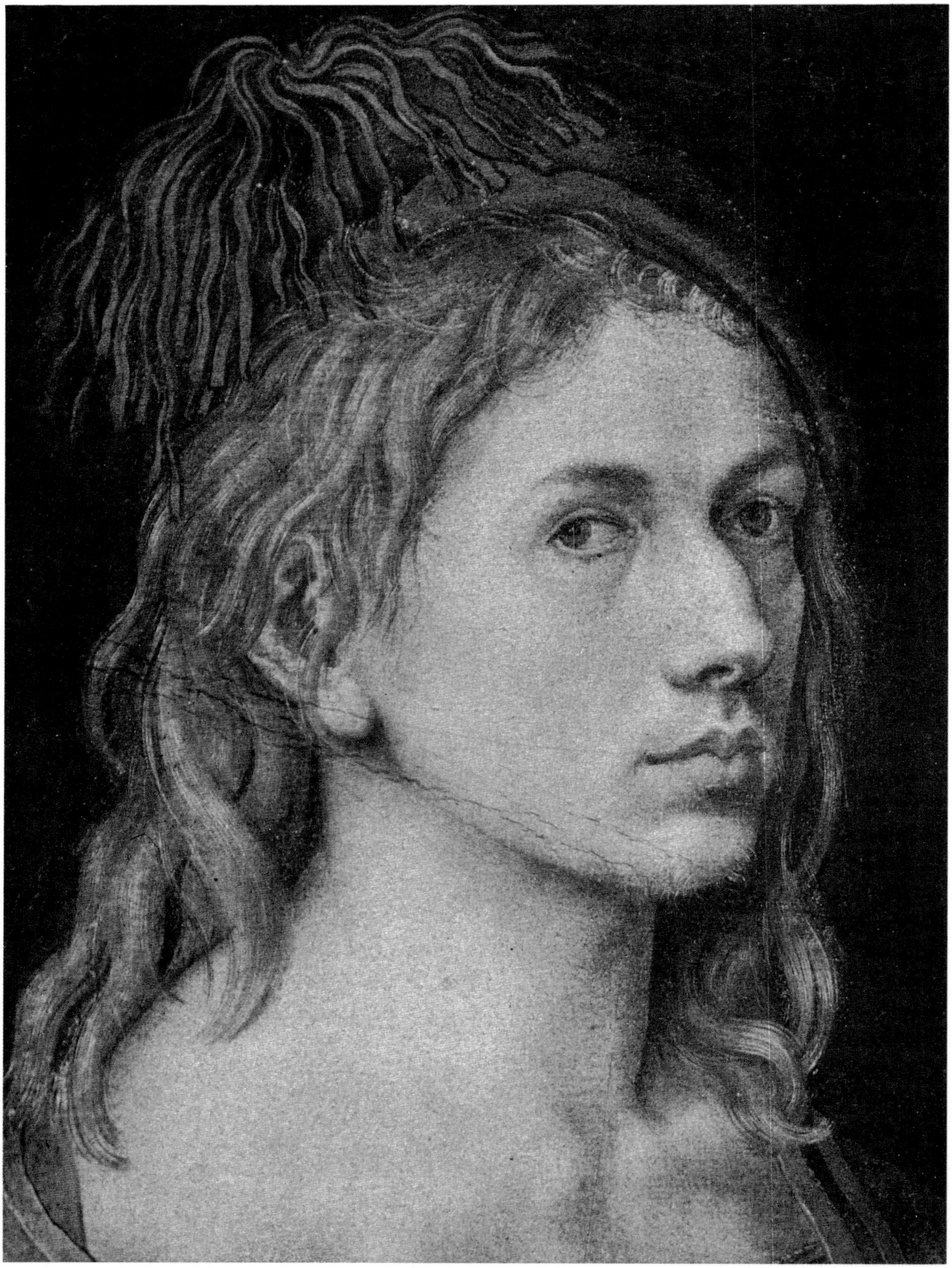

Self-Portrait with Eryngium Flower (Detail)

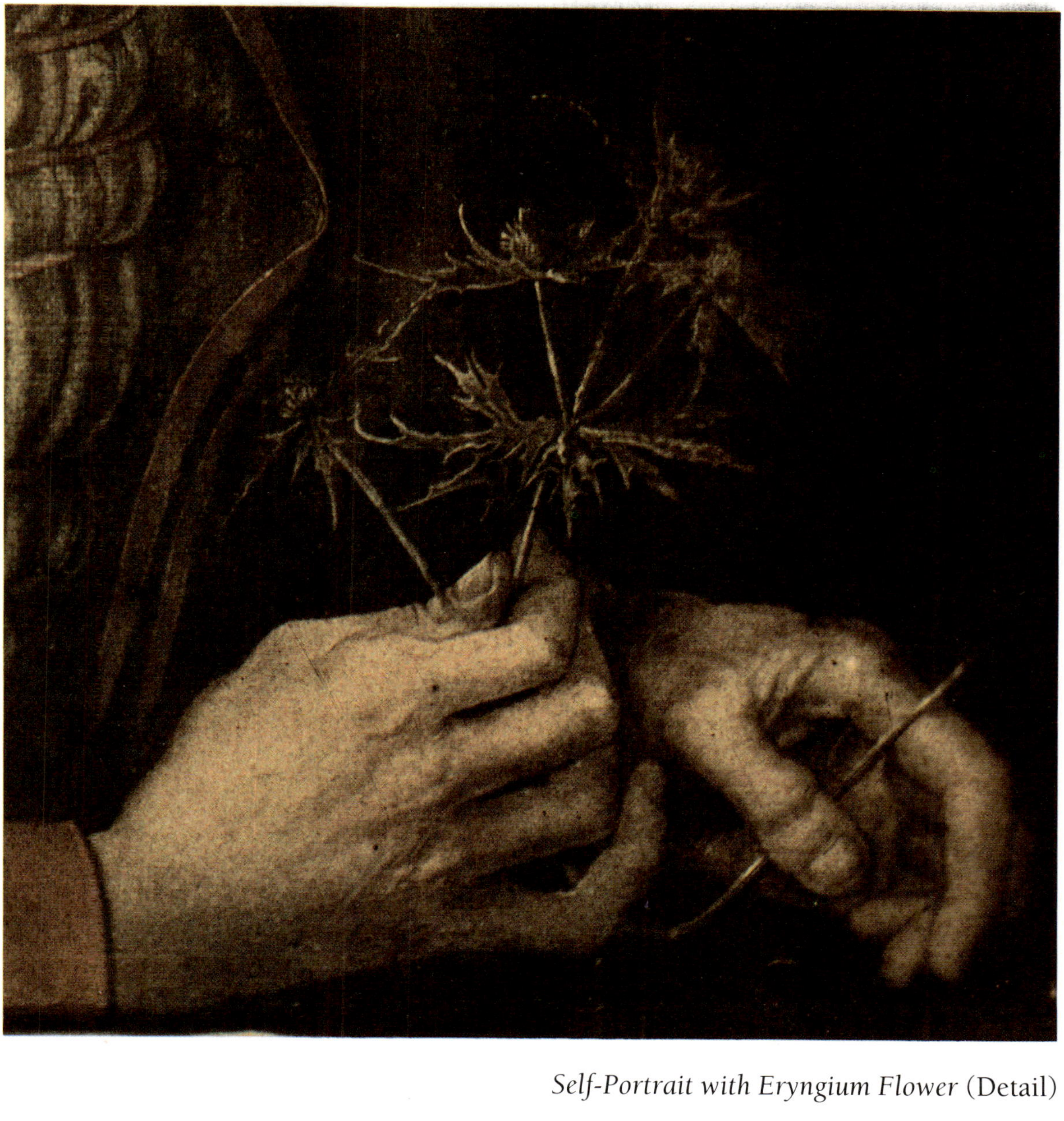

Self-Portrait with Eryngium Flower (Detail)

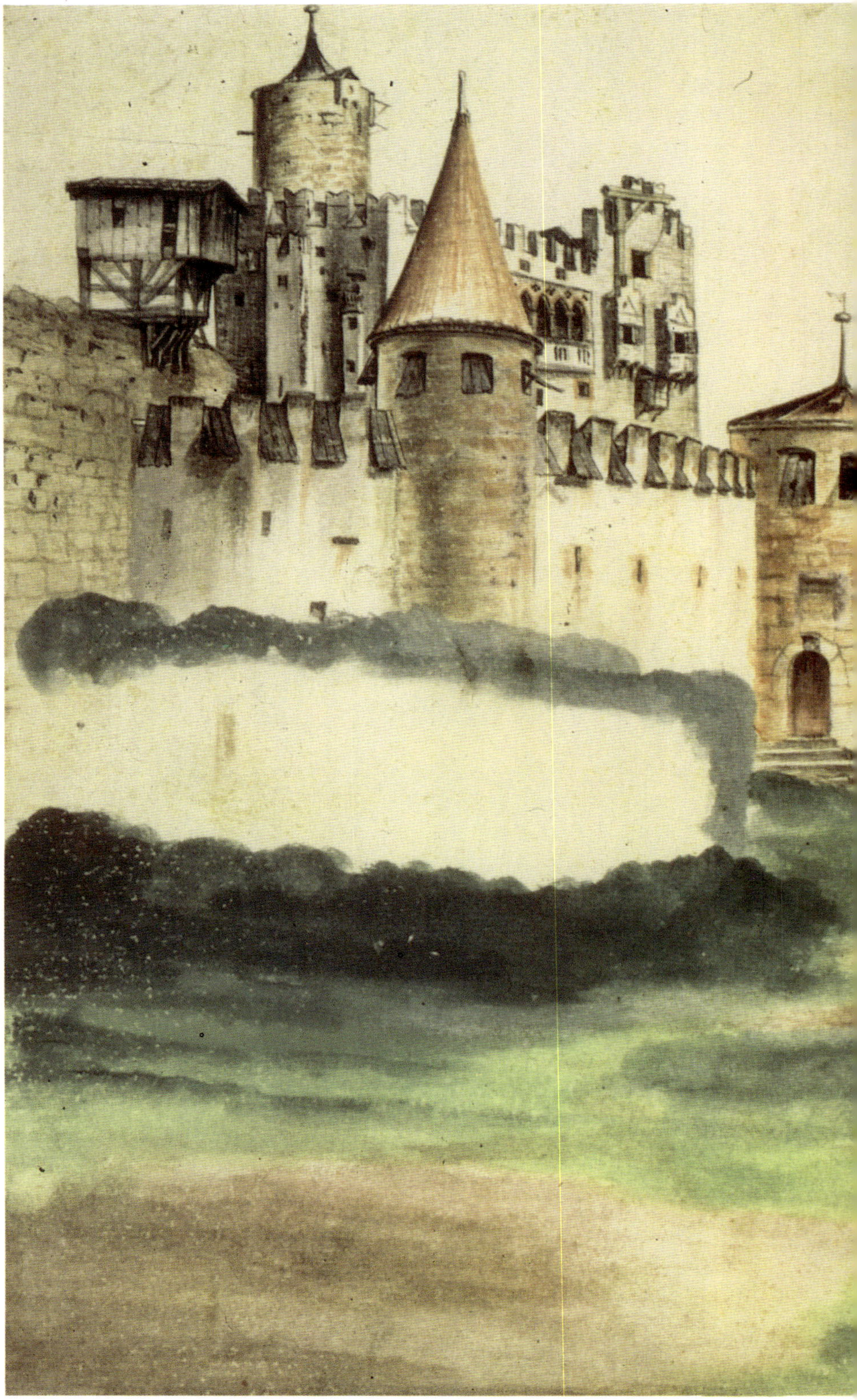

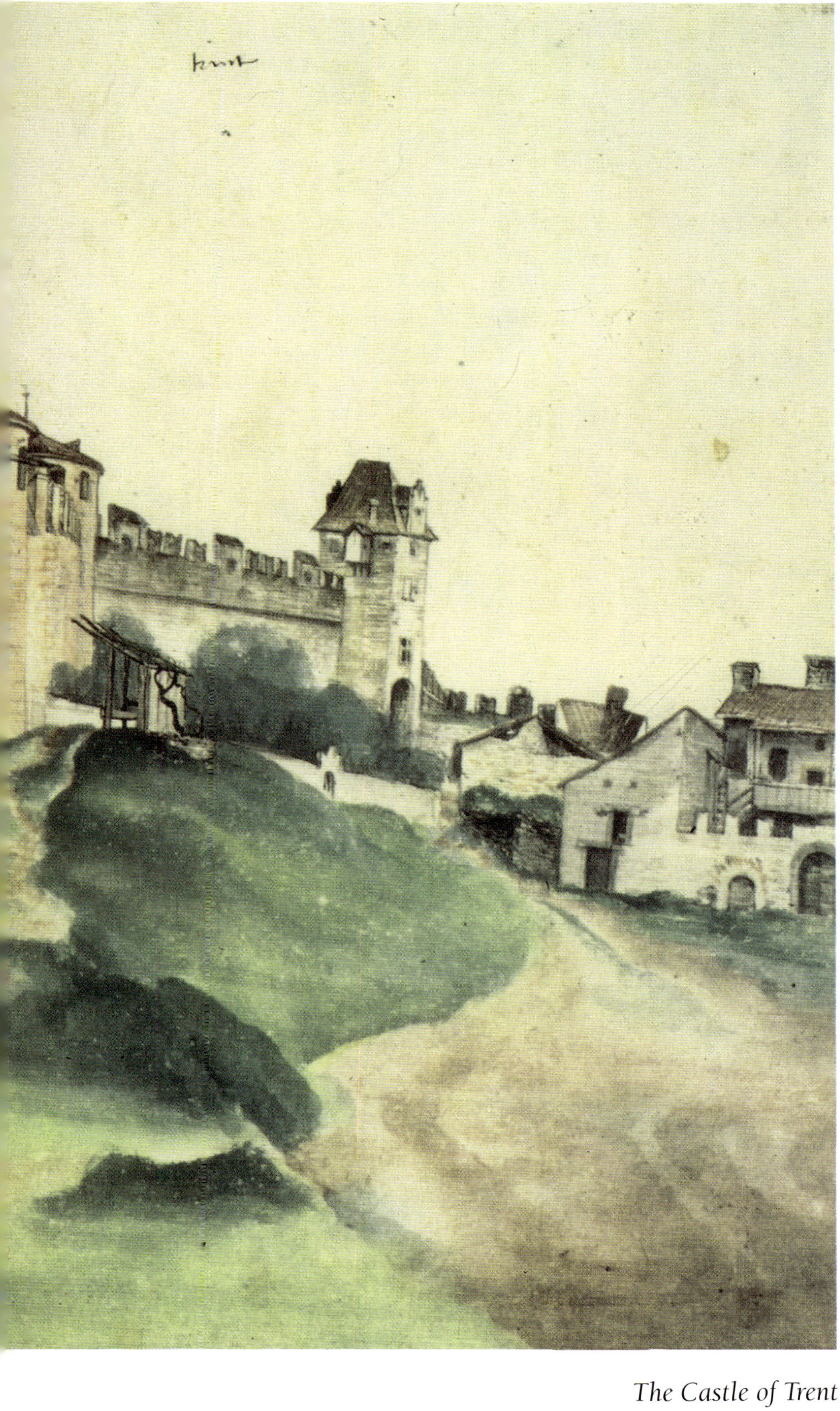

The Castle of Trent

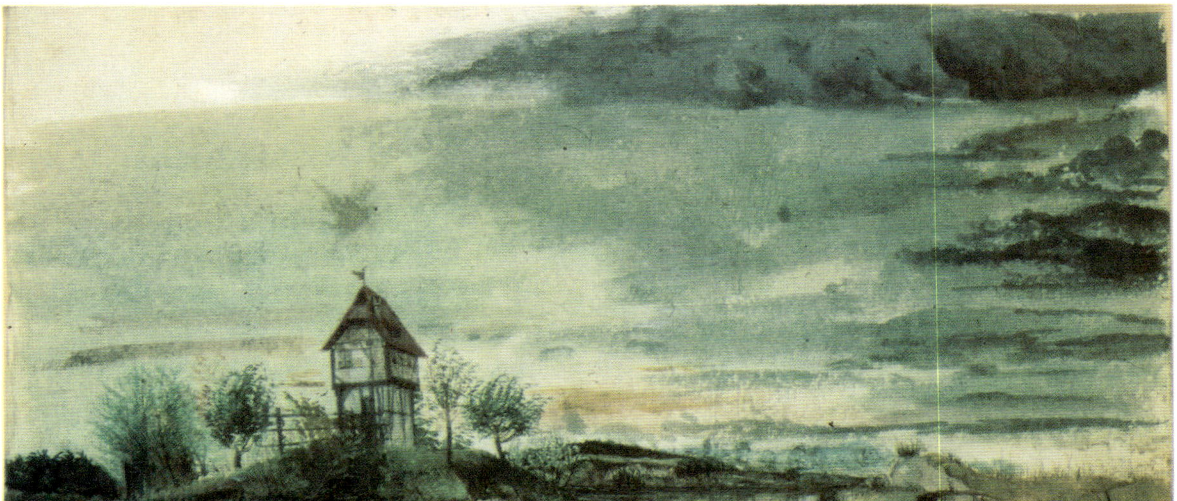

House on an Island in a Pond

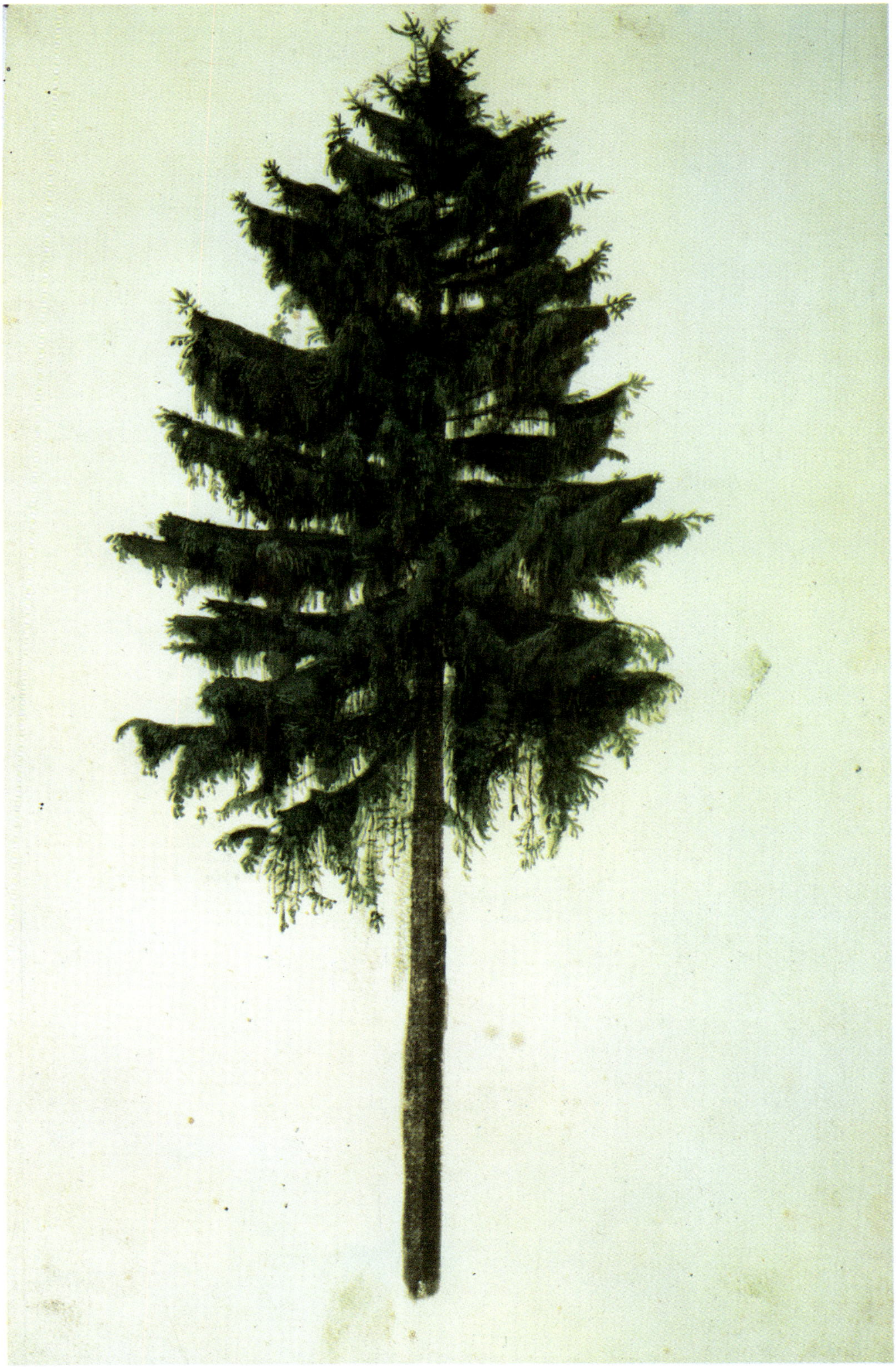

Pine Tree

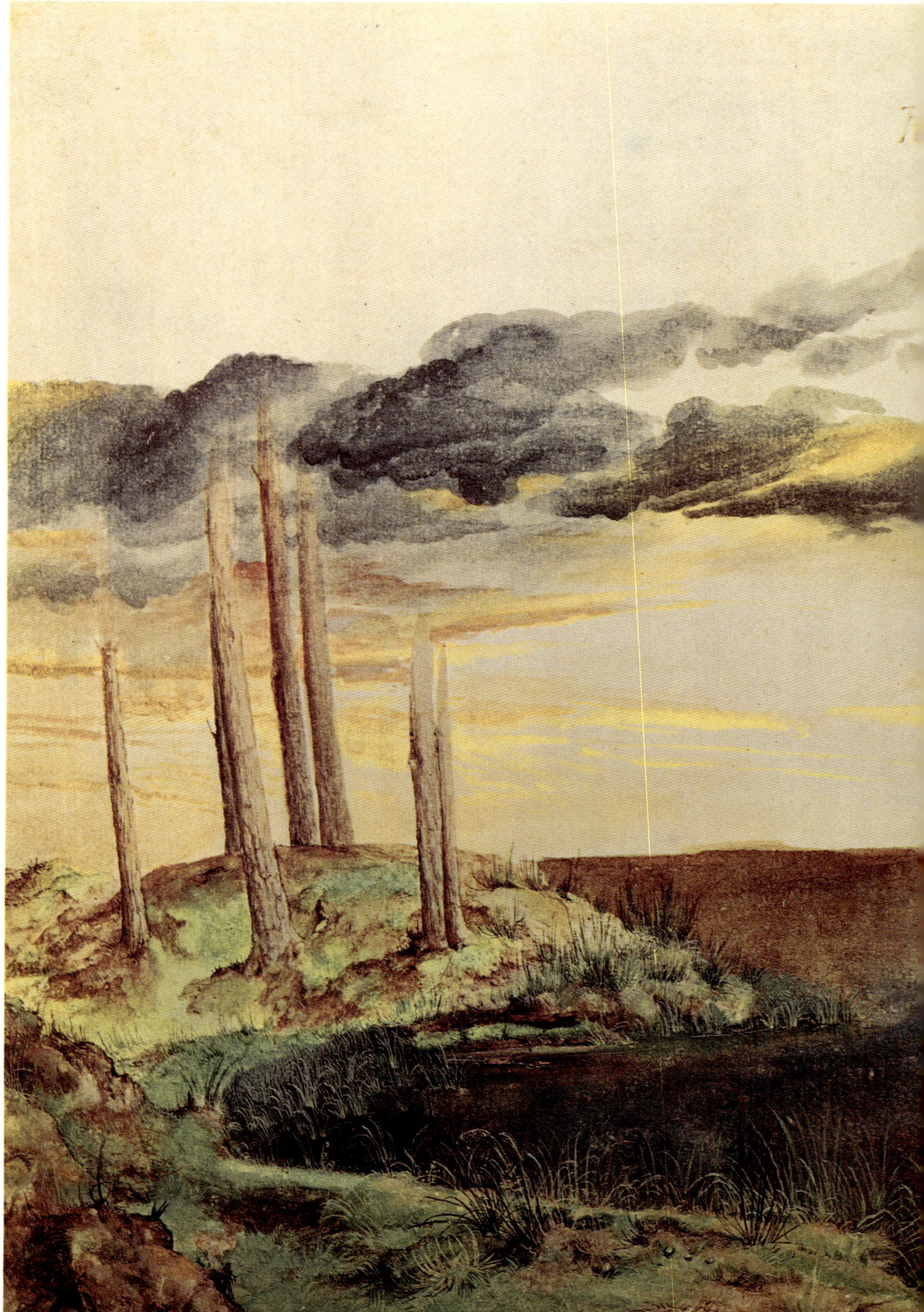

Pond in a Wood

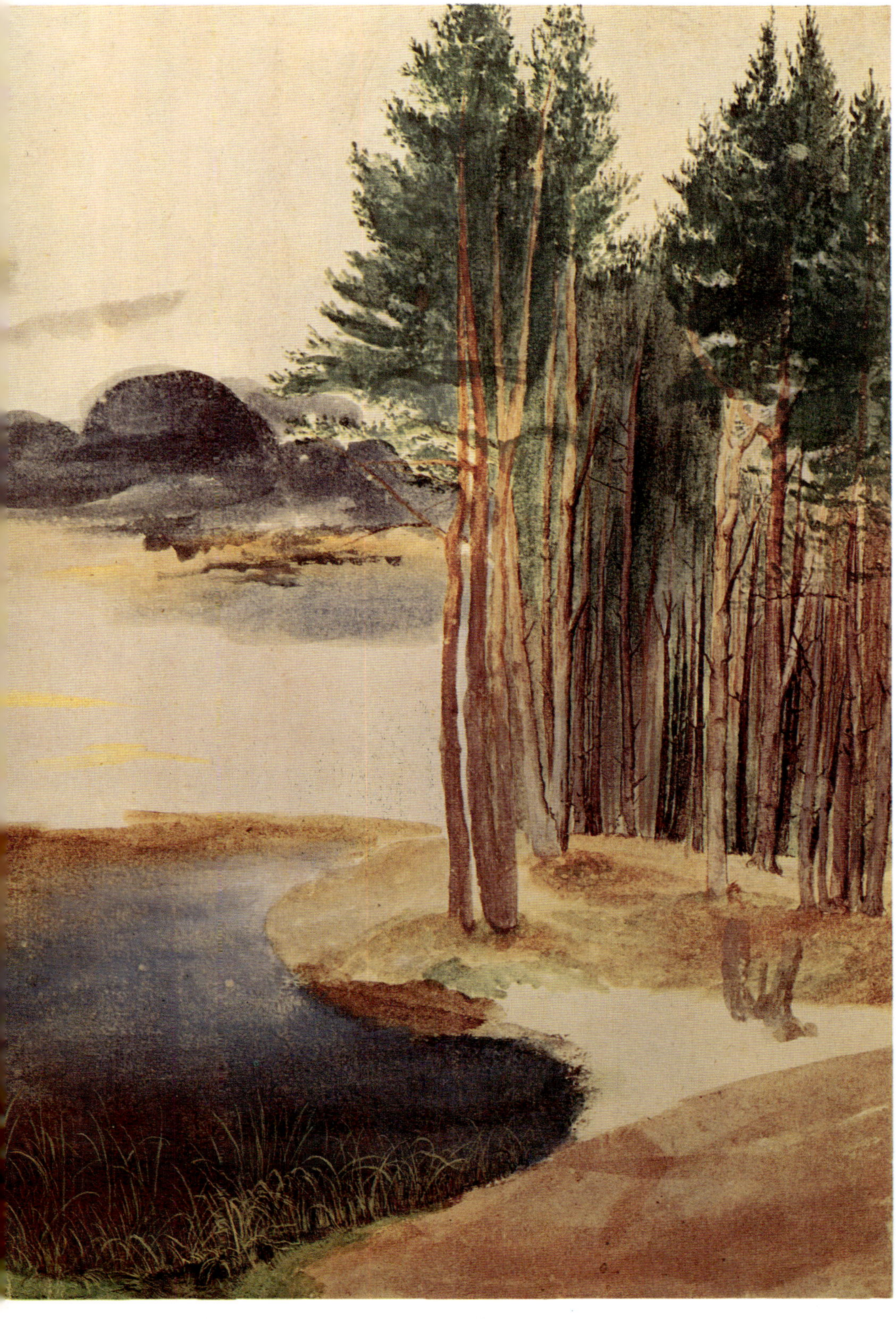

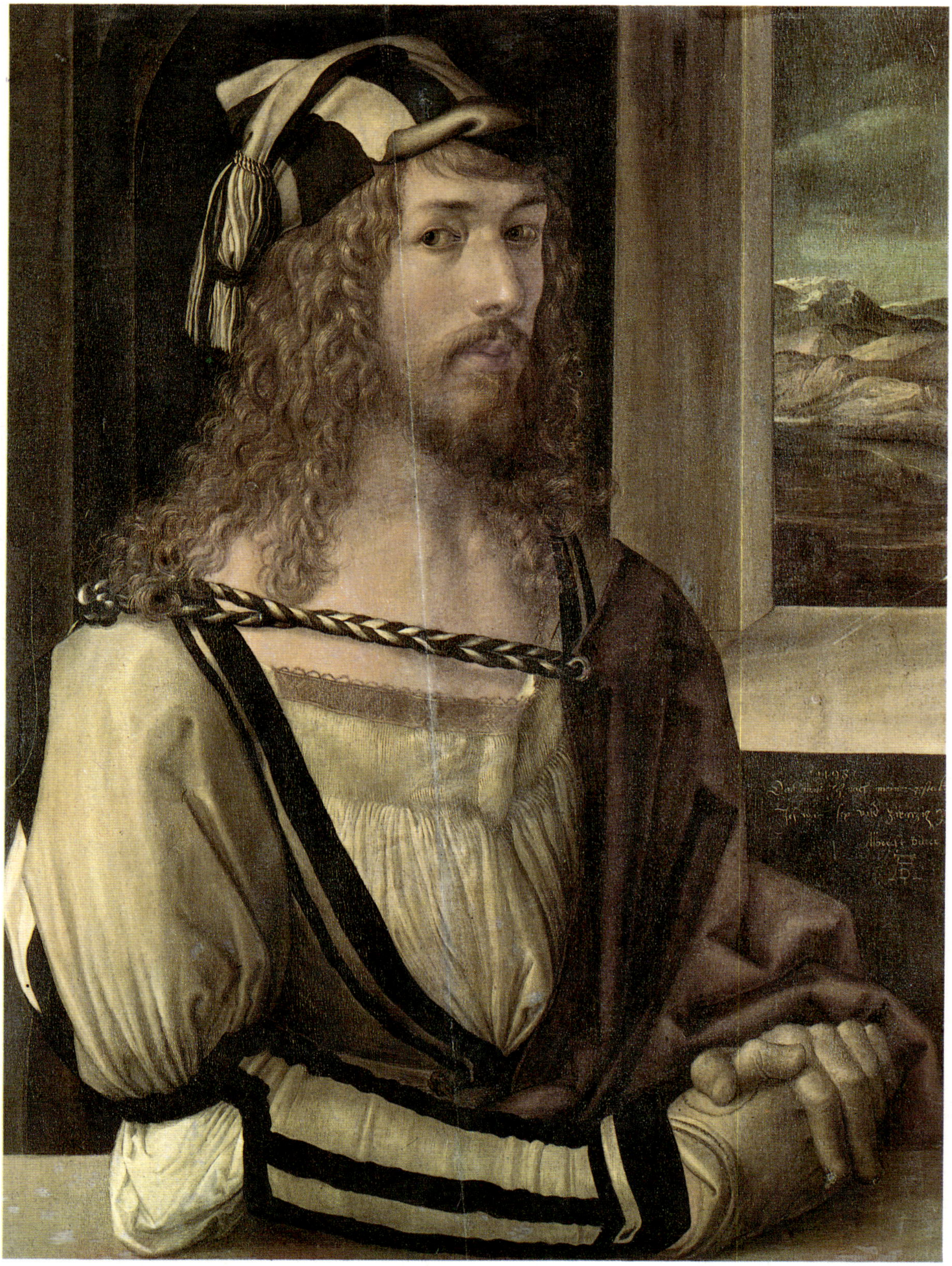

Self-Portrait

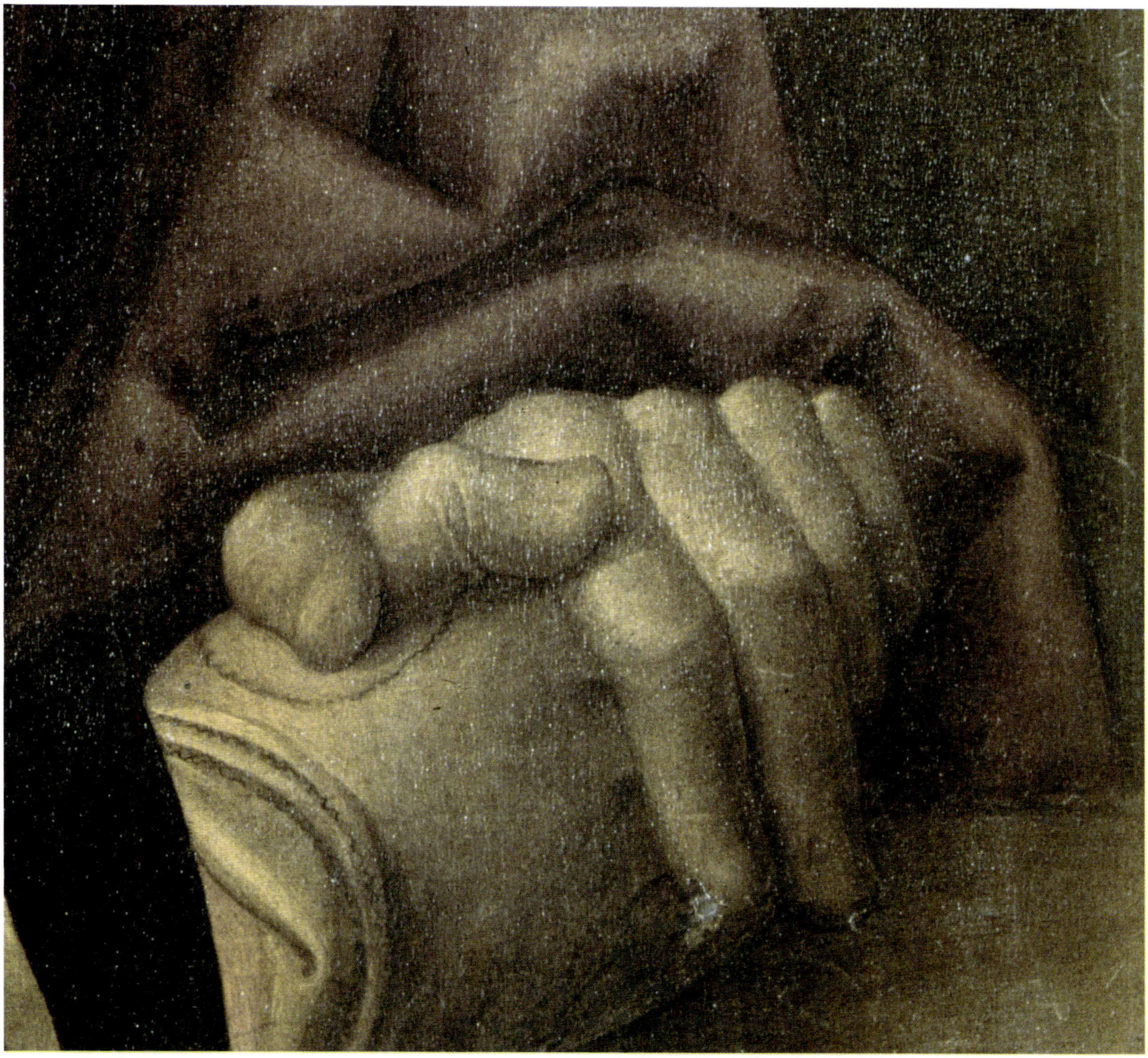

Self-Portrait (Detail)

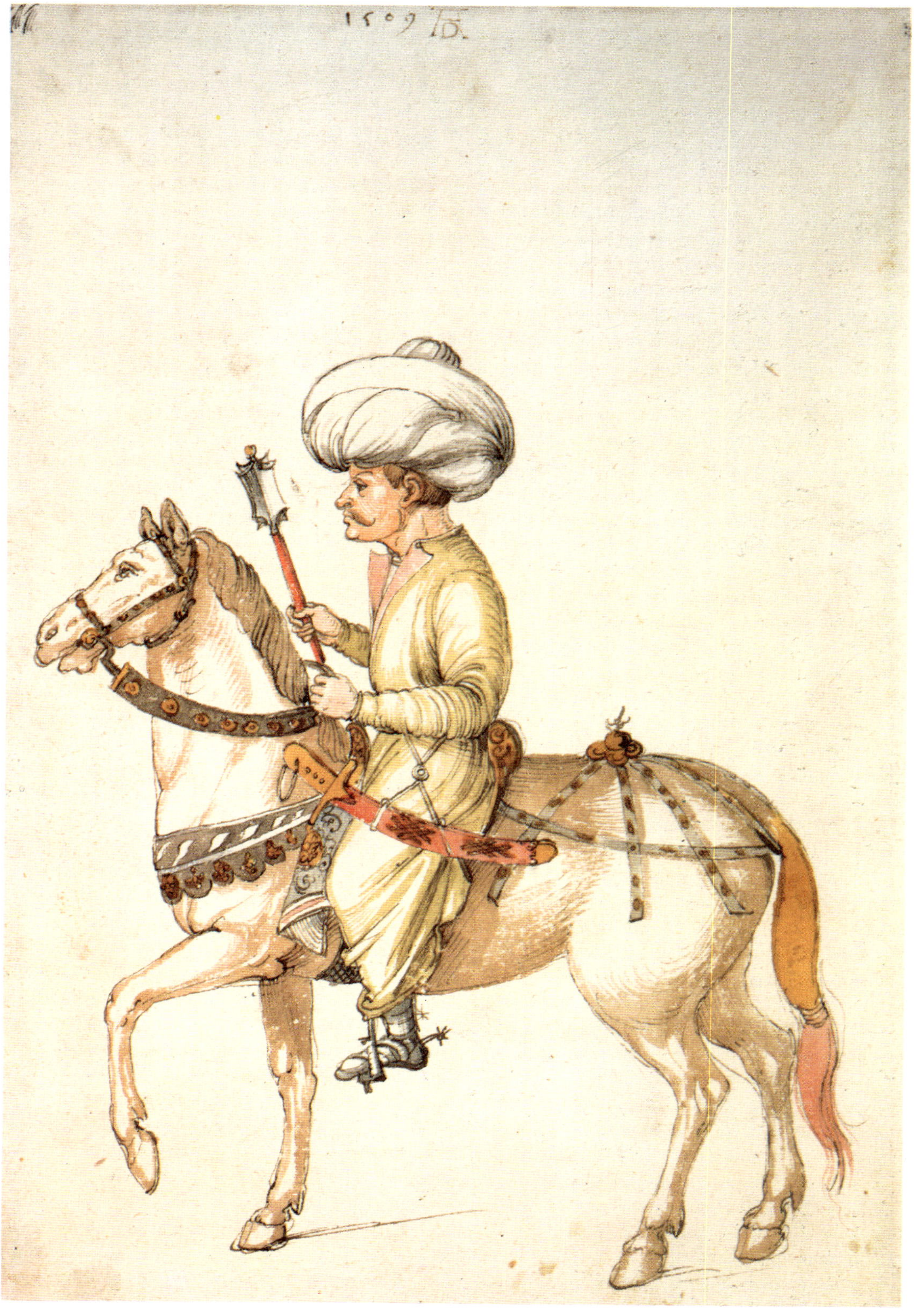

Turkish Horseman

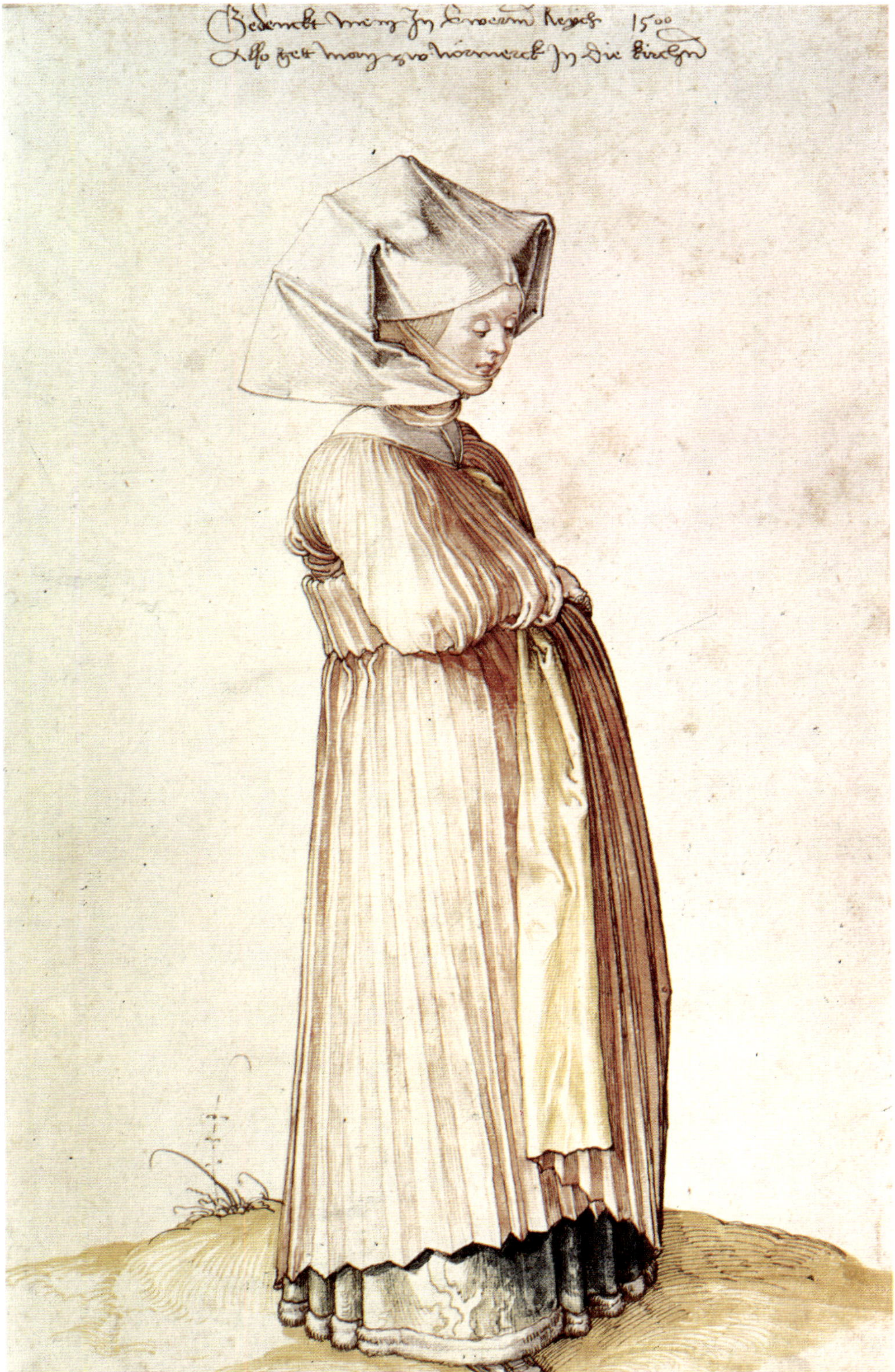

Nuremburg Woman Dressed for Church

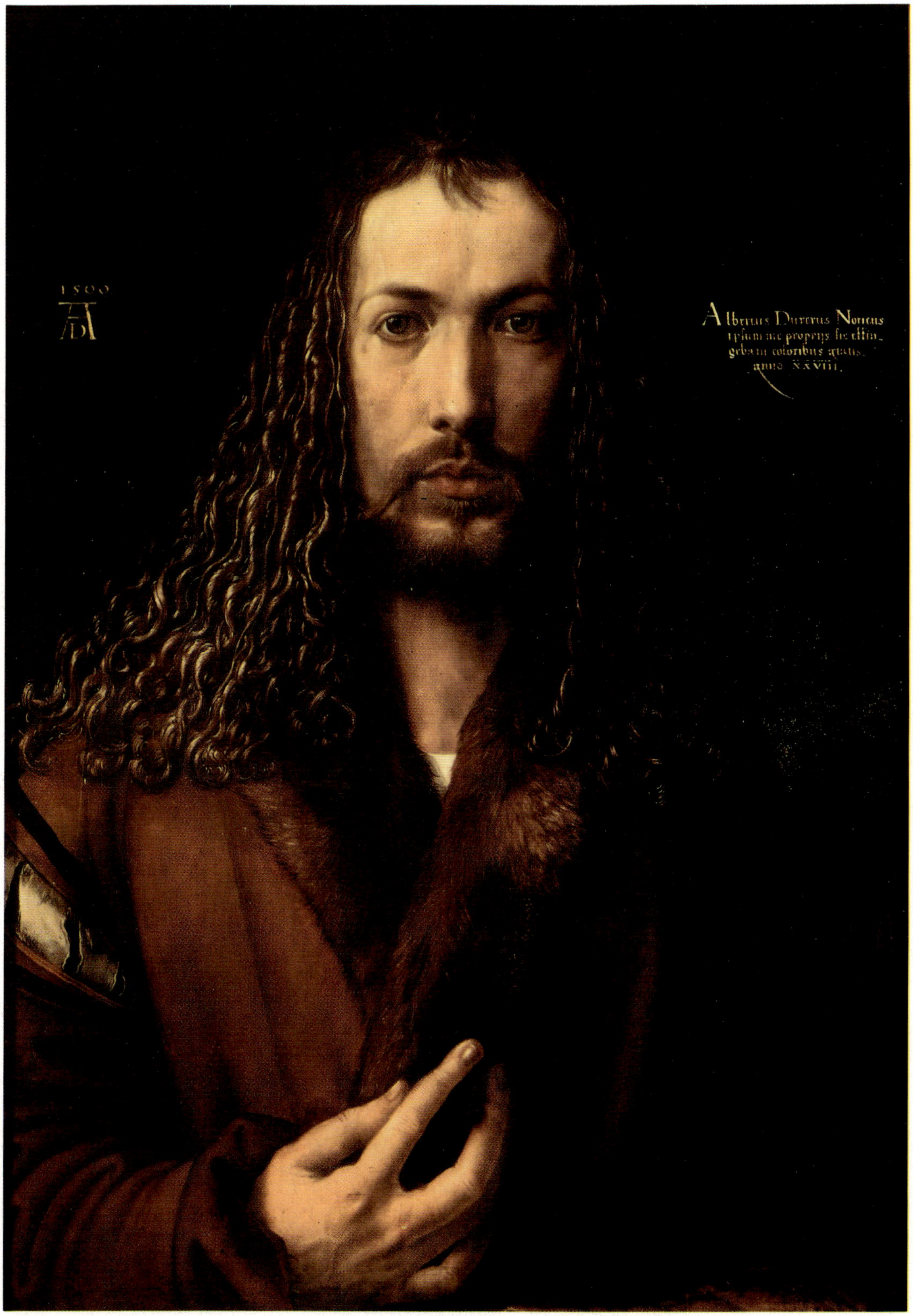

Self-Portrait

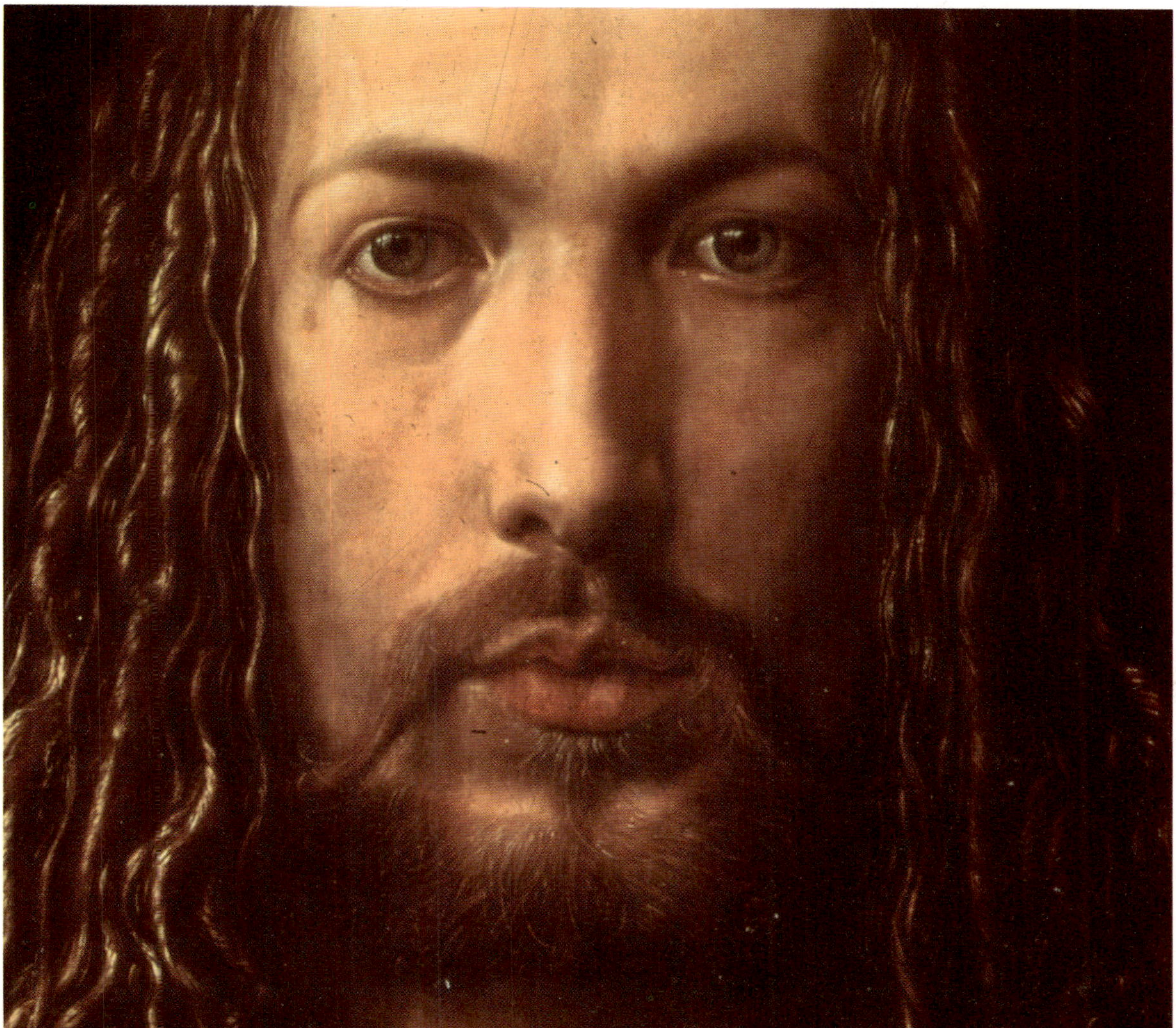

Self-Portrait (Detail)

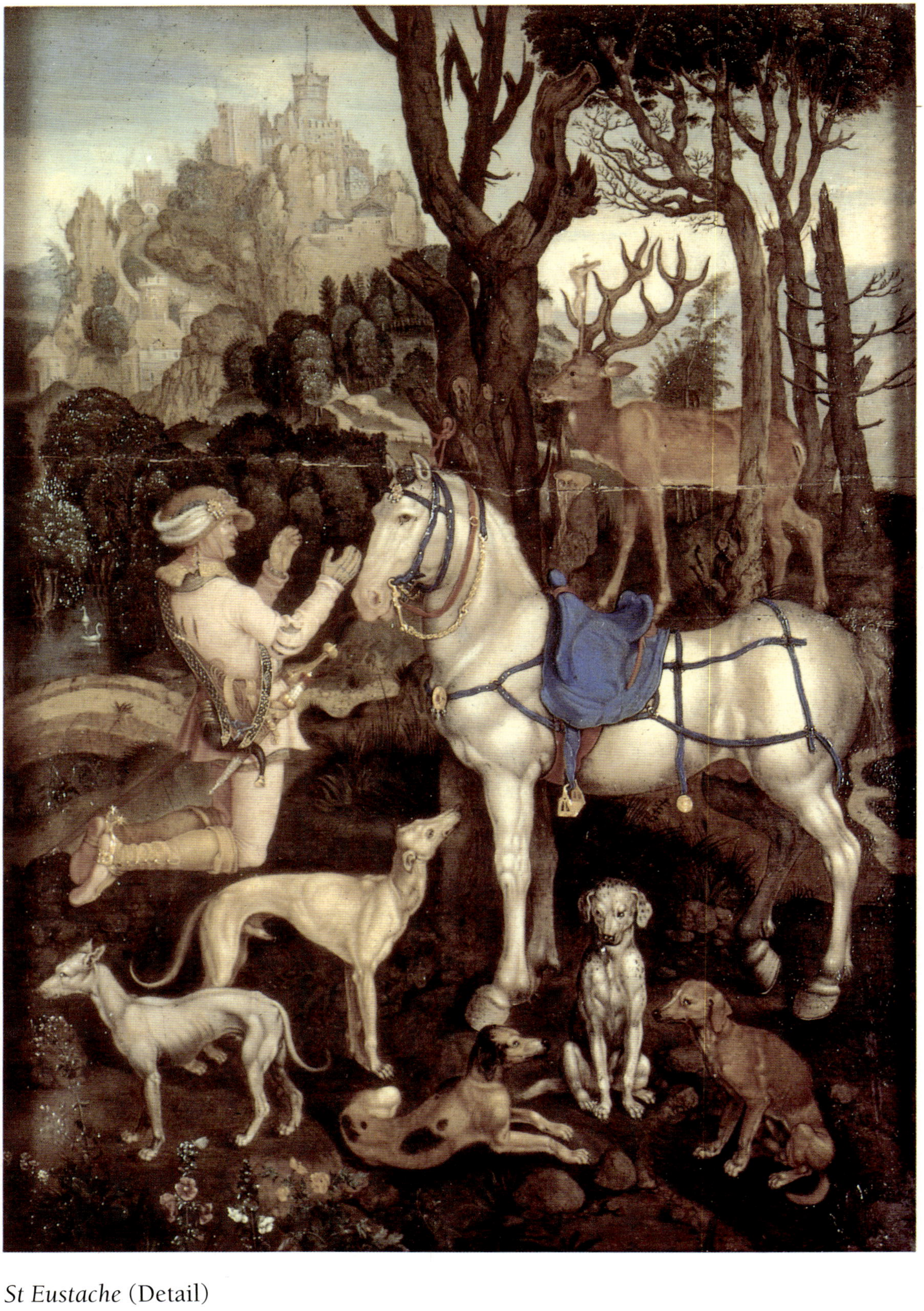

St Eustache (Detail)

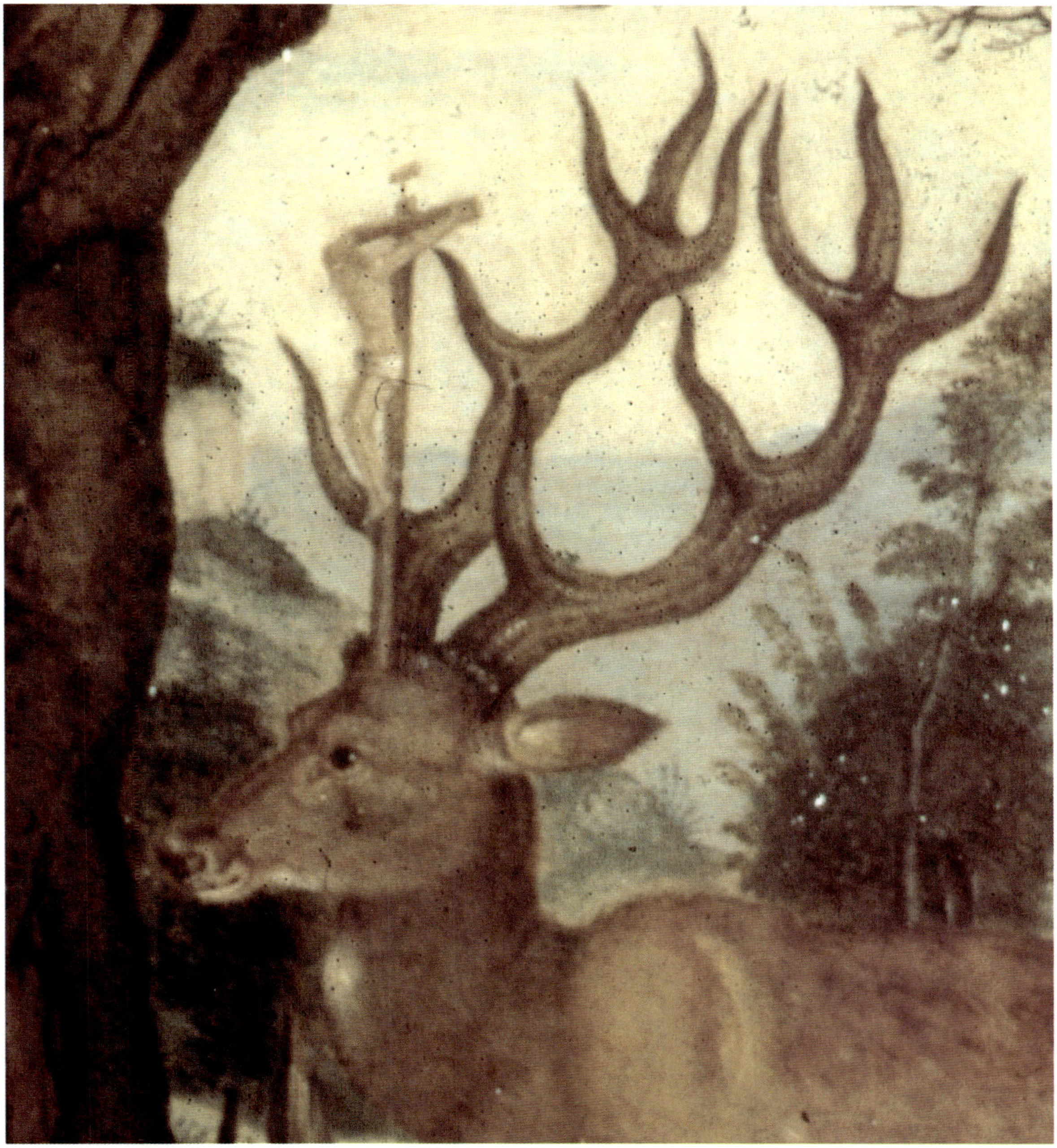

St Eustache (Detail)

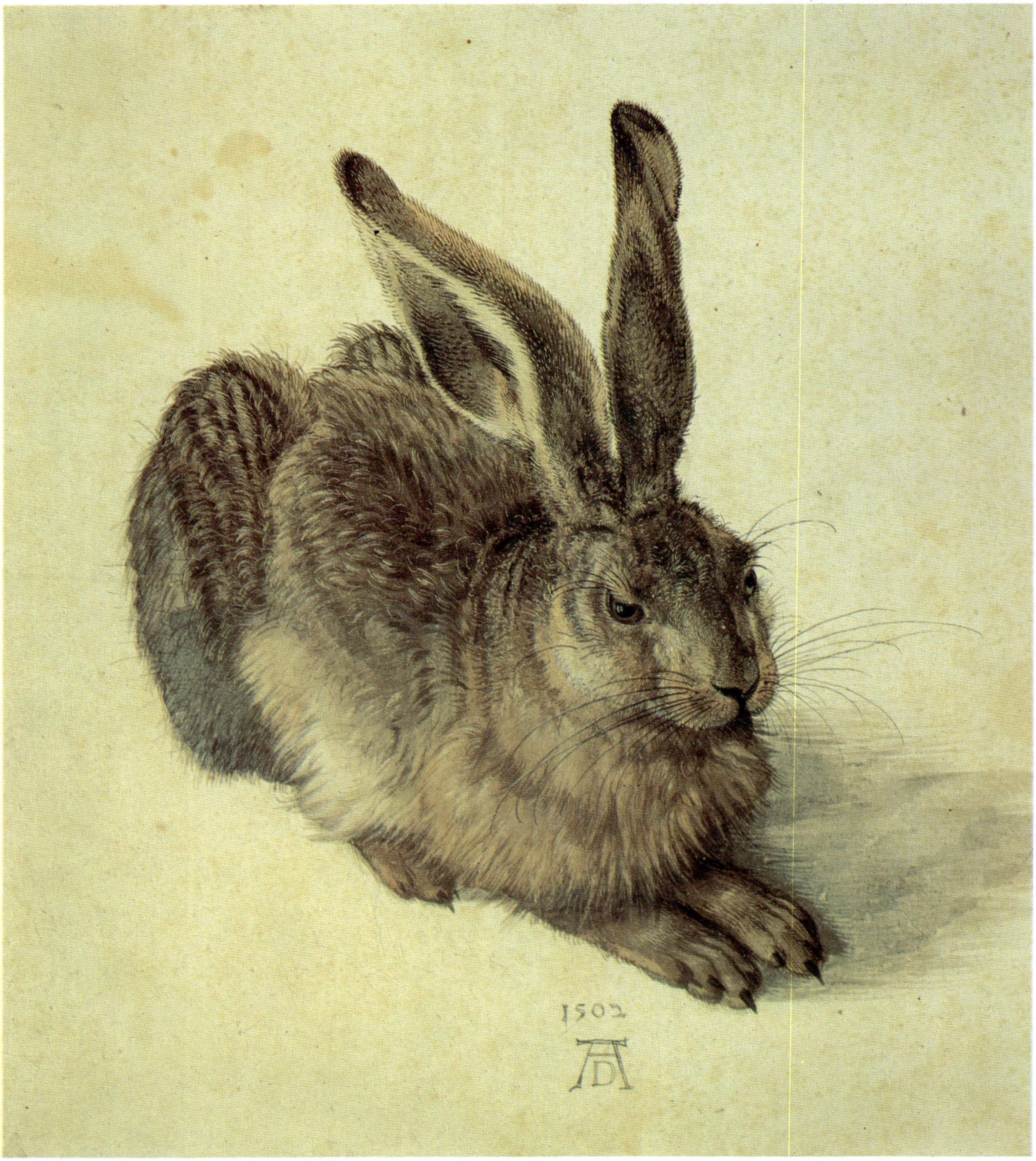

Young Hare

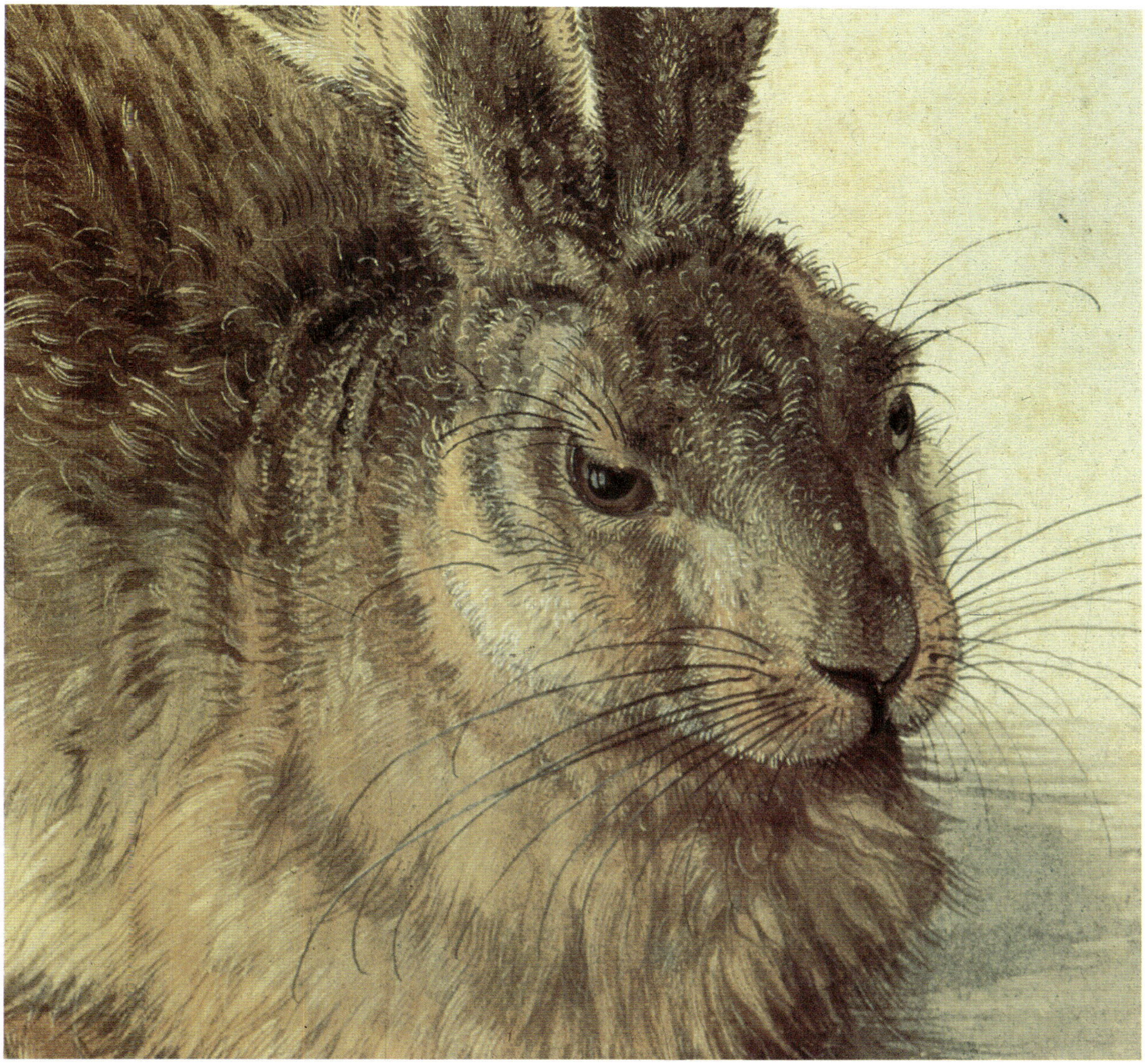

Young Hare (Detail)

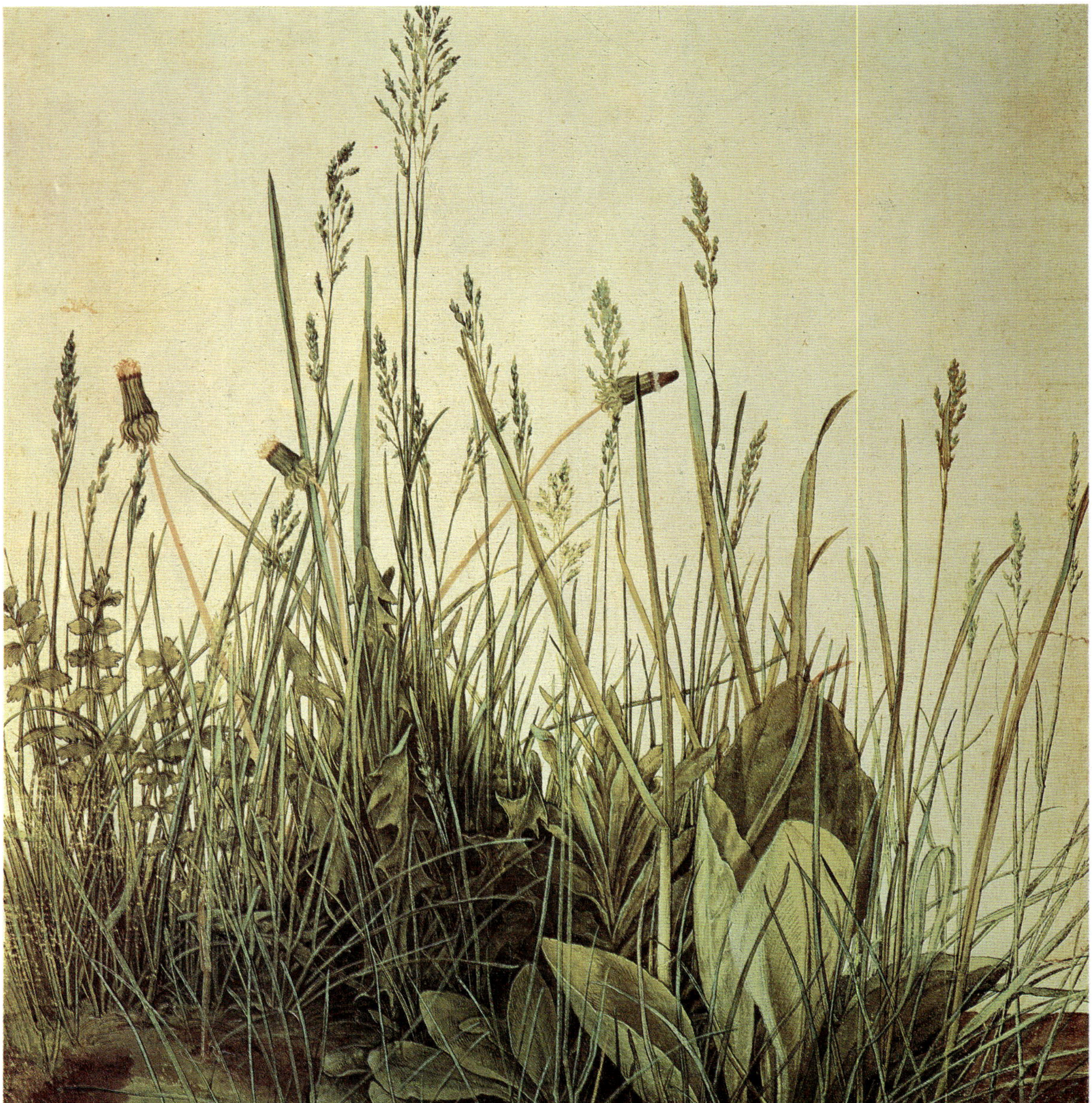

Great Piece of Turf

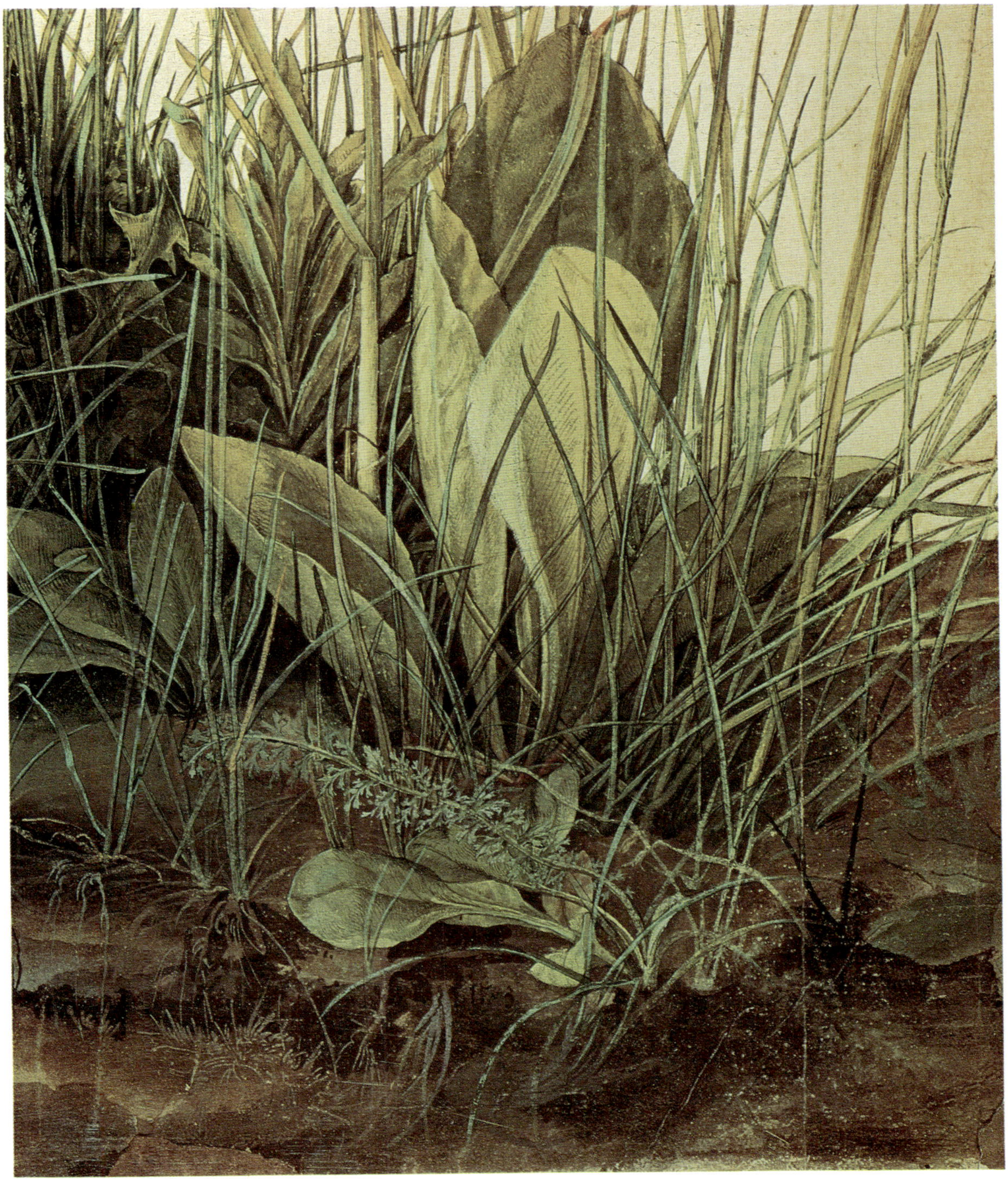

Great Piece of Turf (Detail)

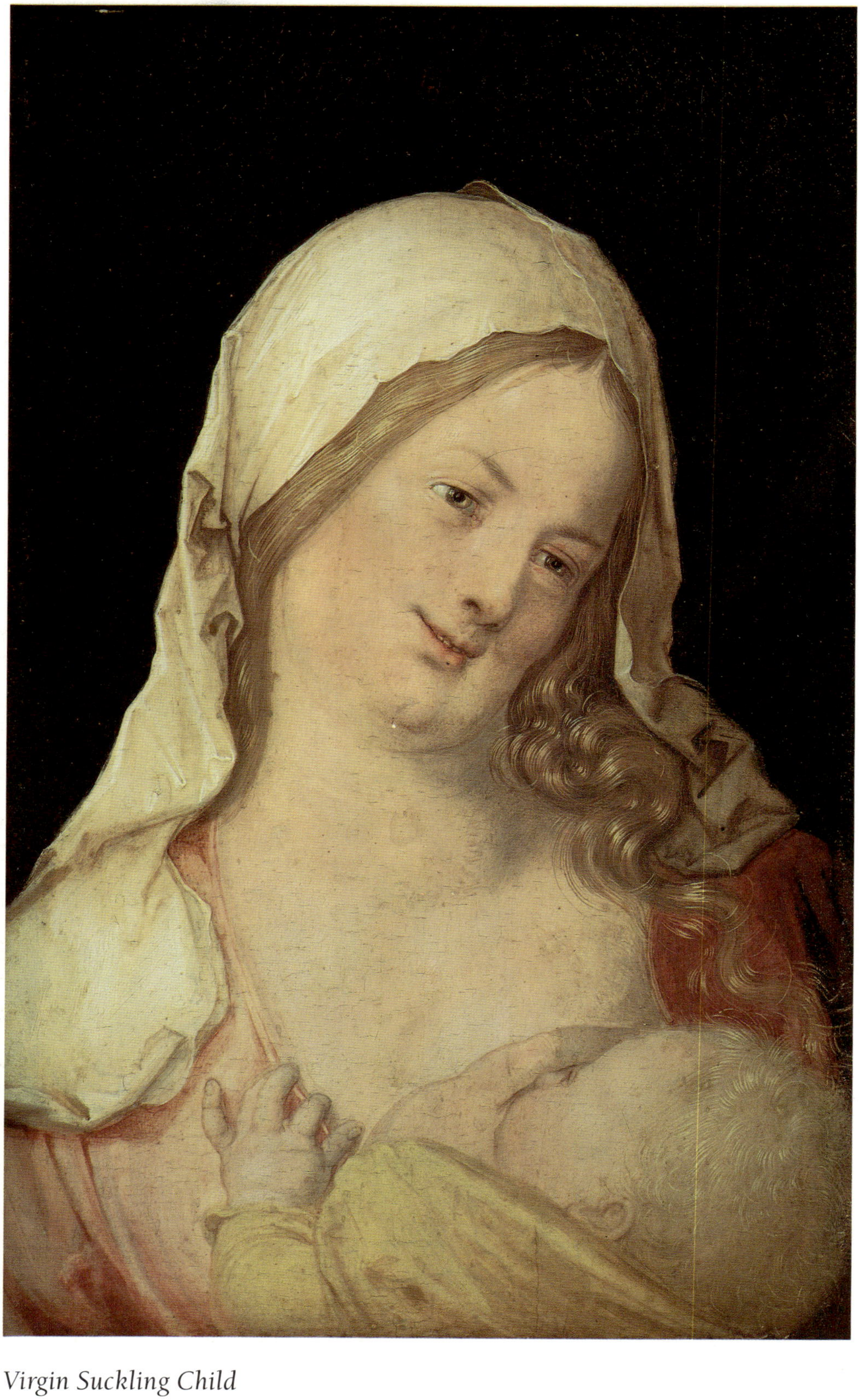

Virgin Suckling Child

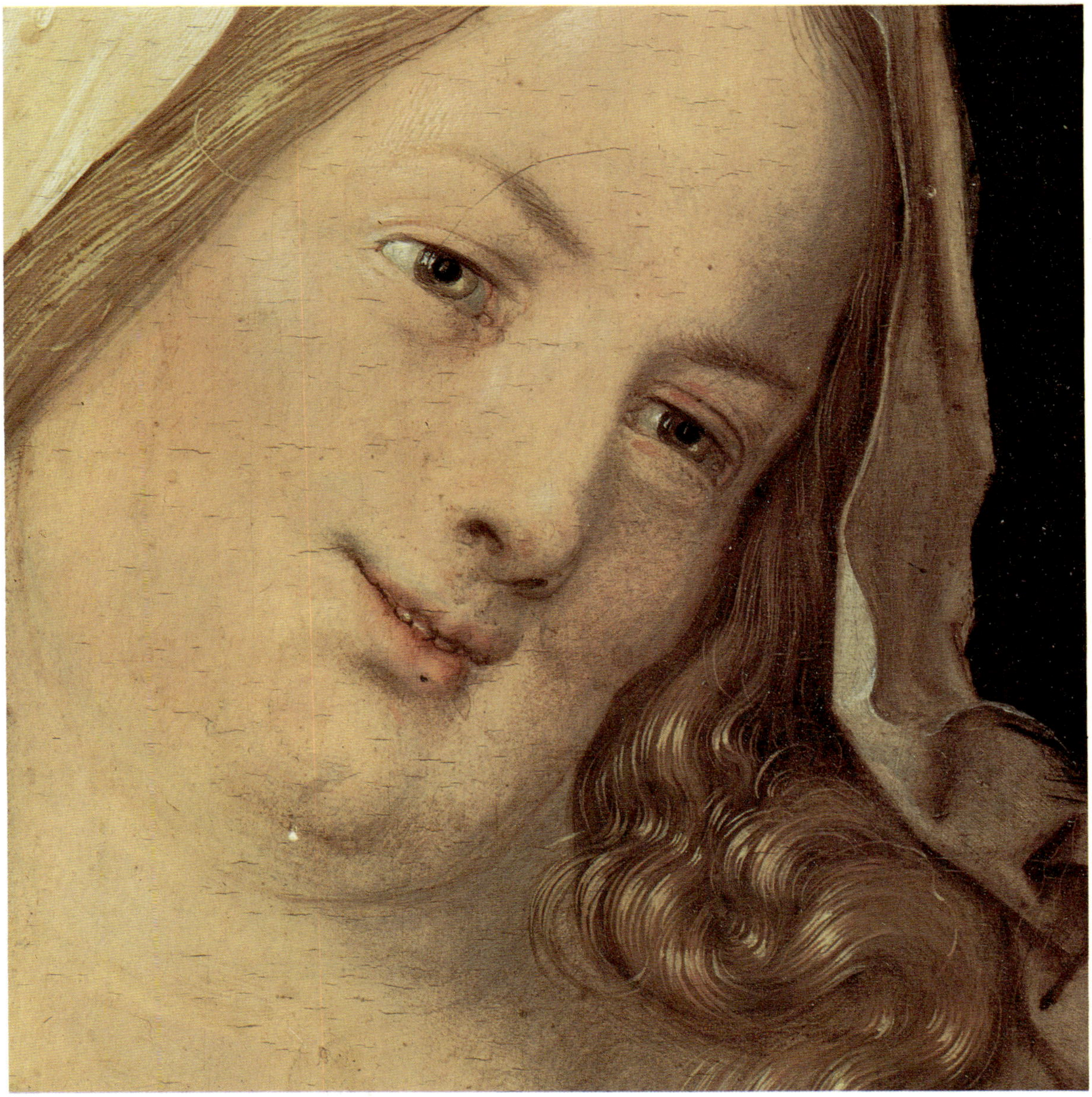

Virgin Suckling Child (Detail)

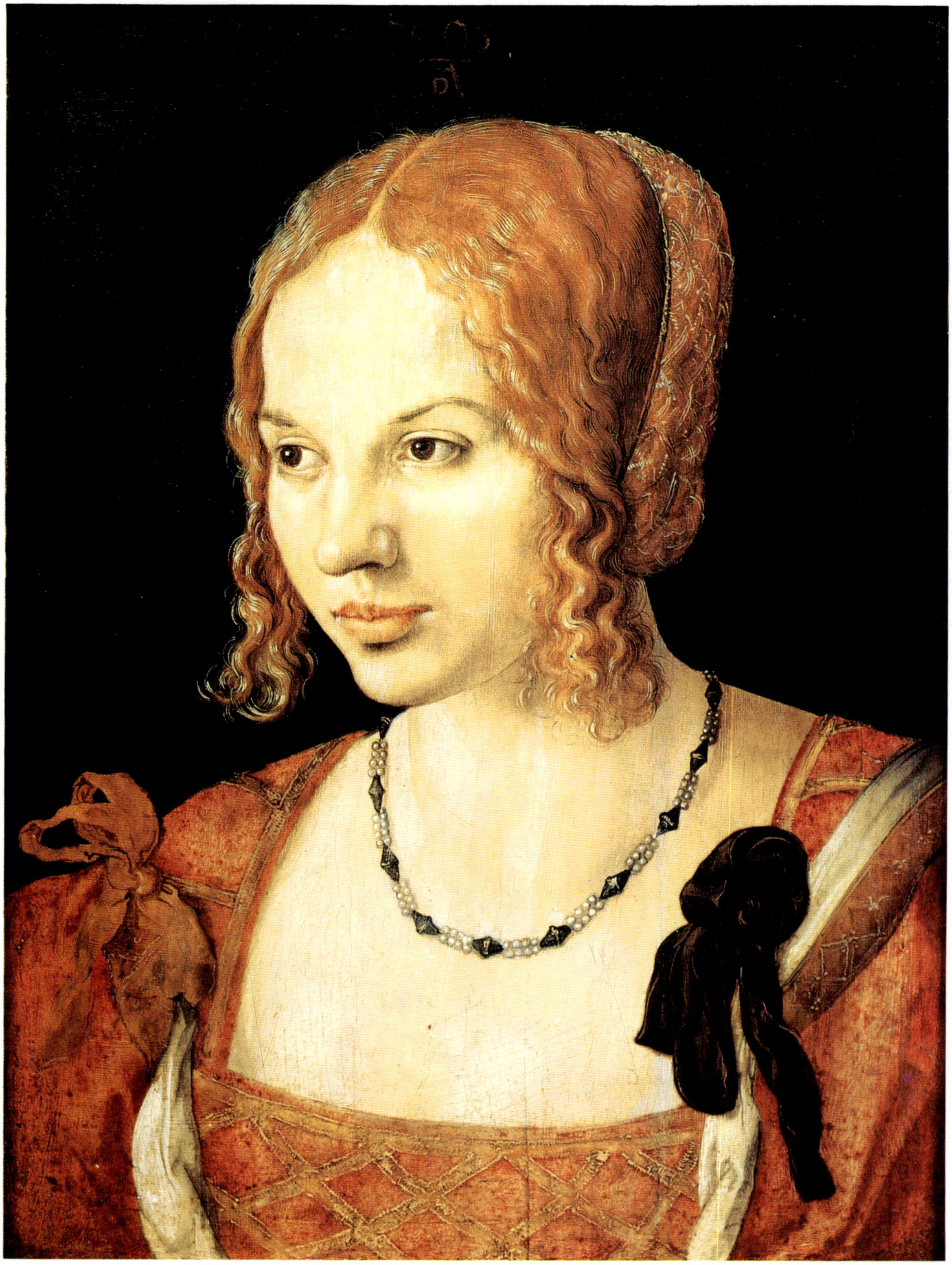

Portrait of a Venetian Girl

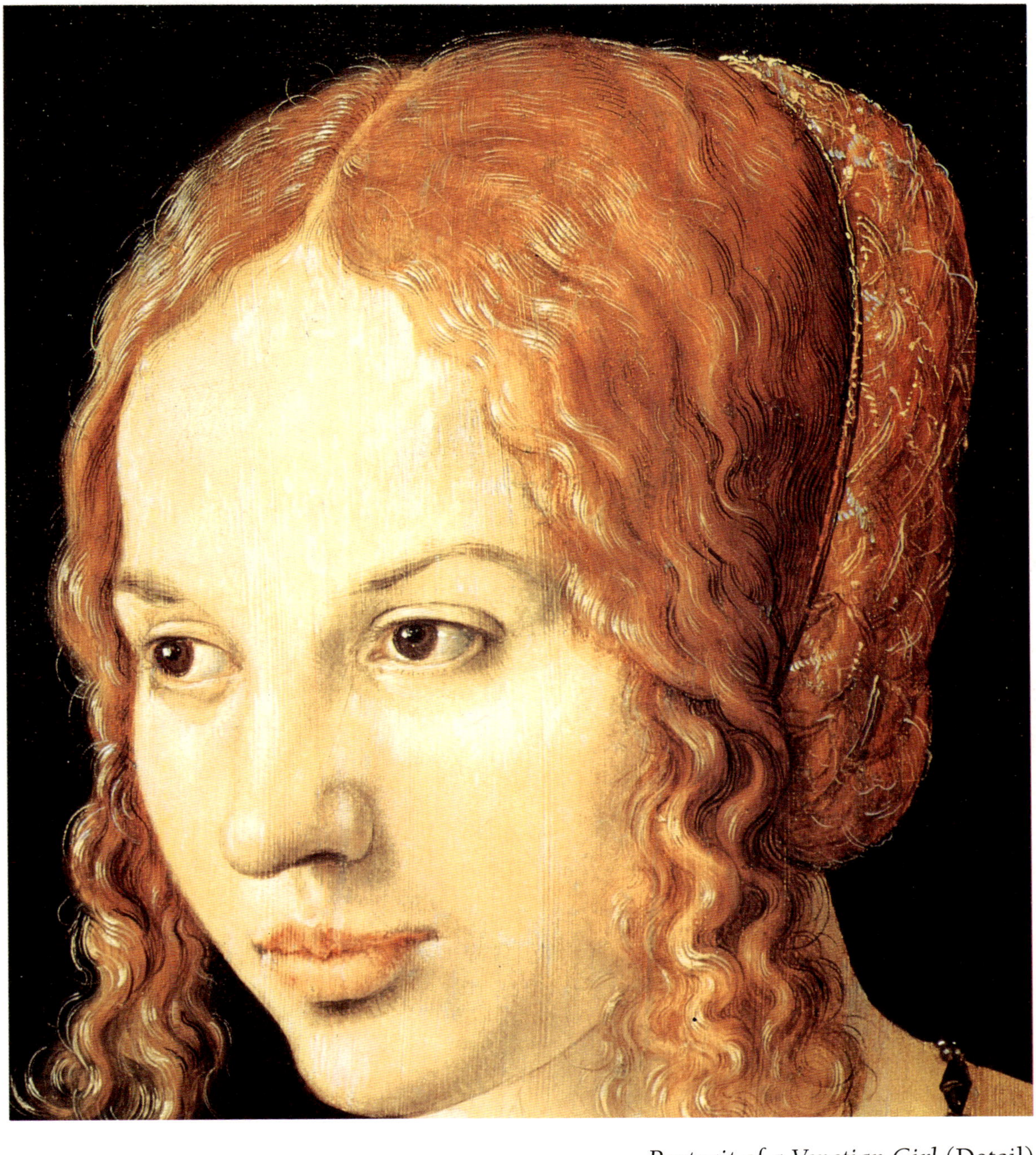

Portrait of a Venetian Girl (Detail)

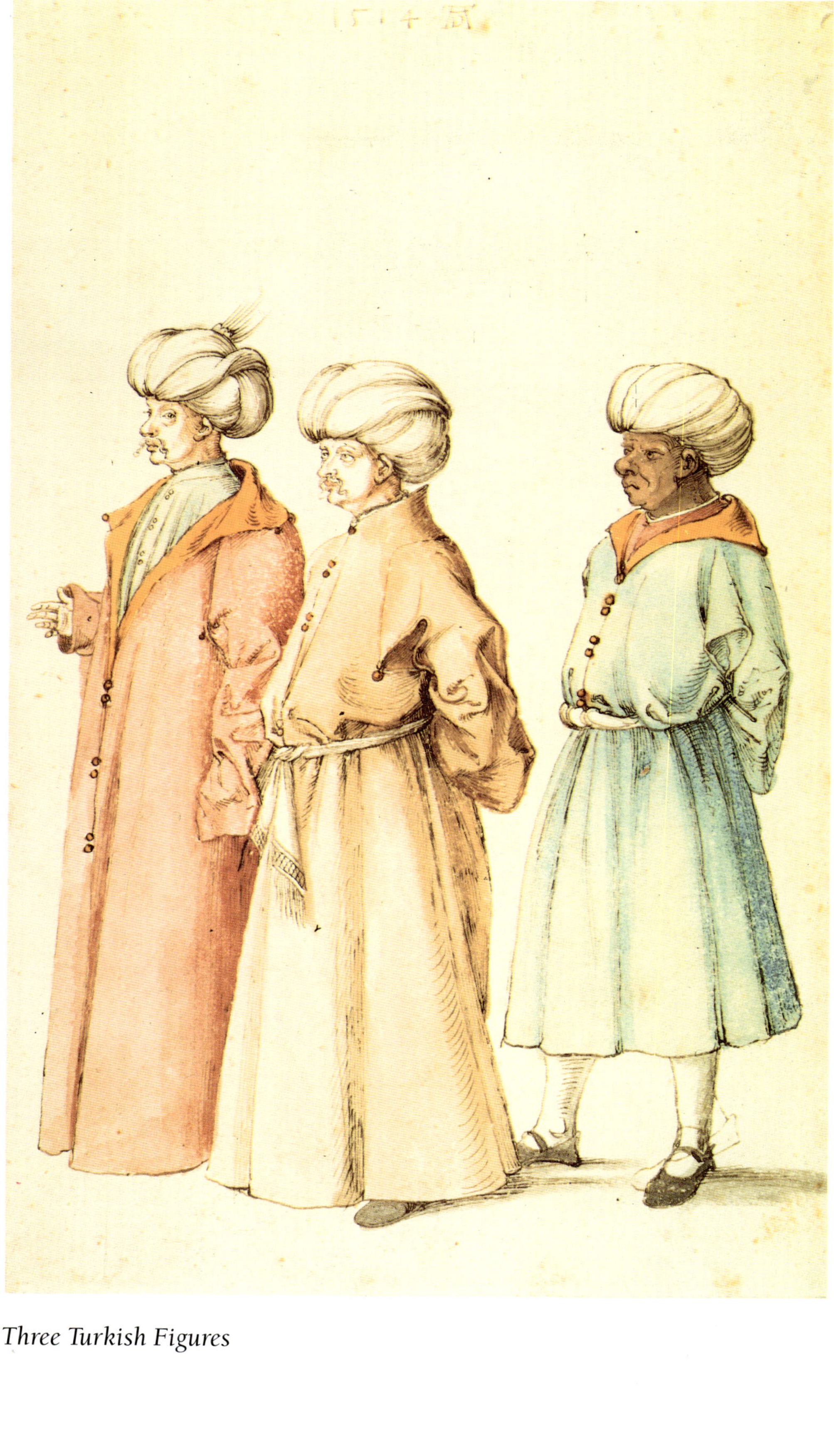

Three Turkish Figures

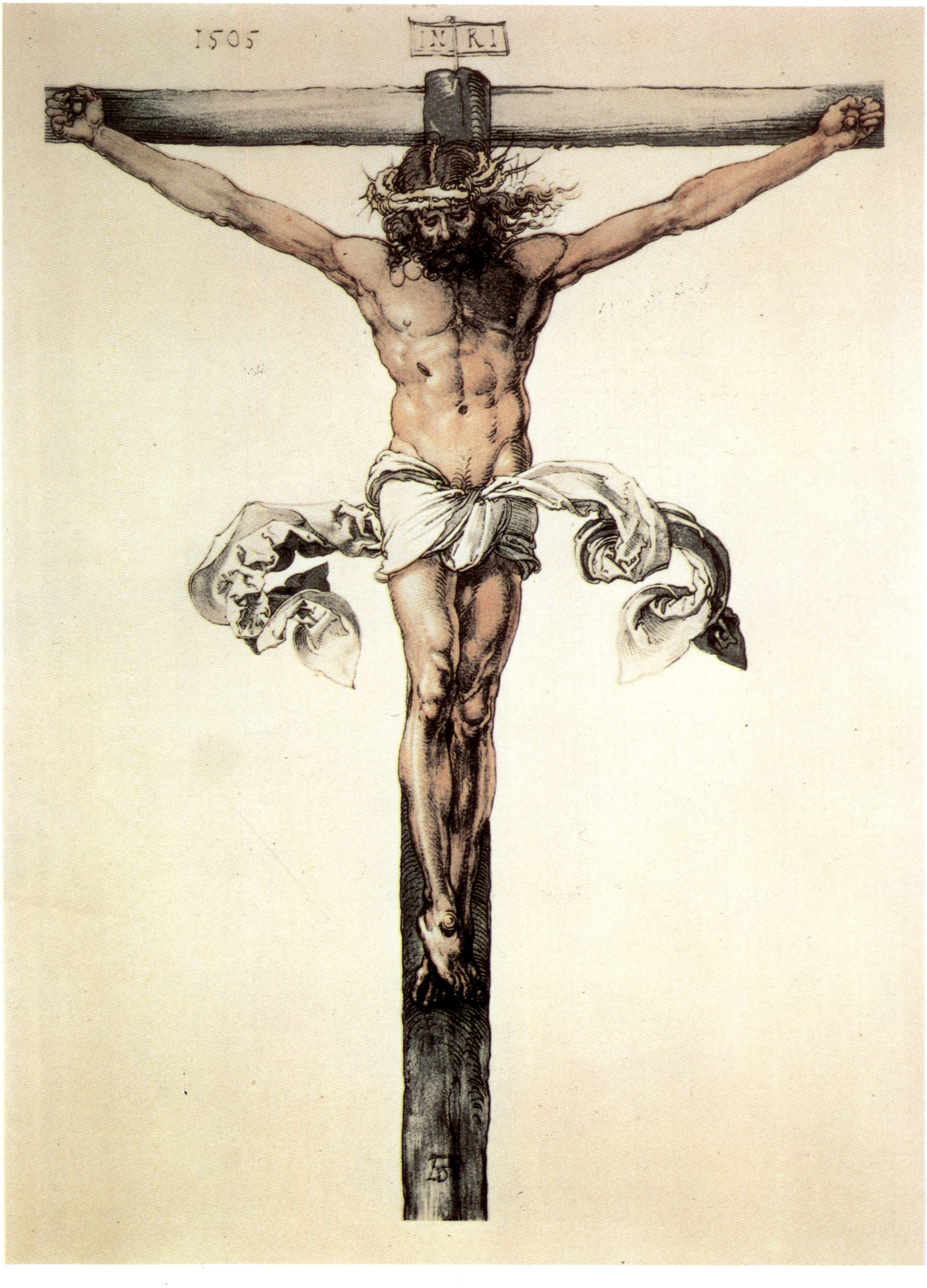

Christ on the Cross

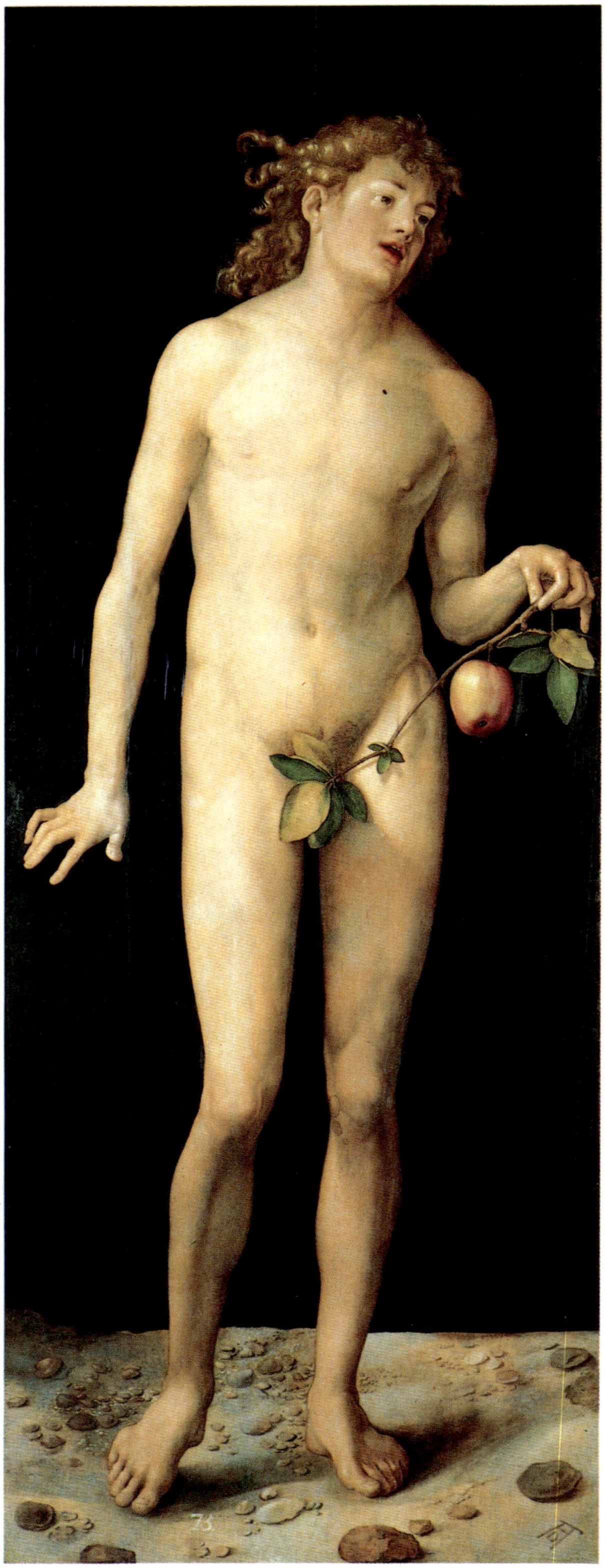

Adam

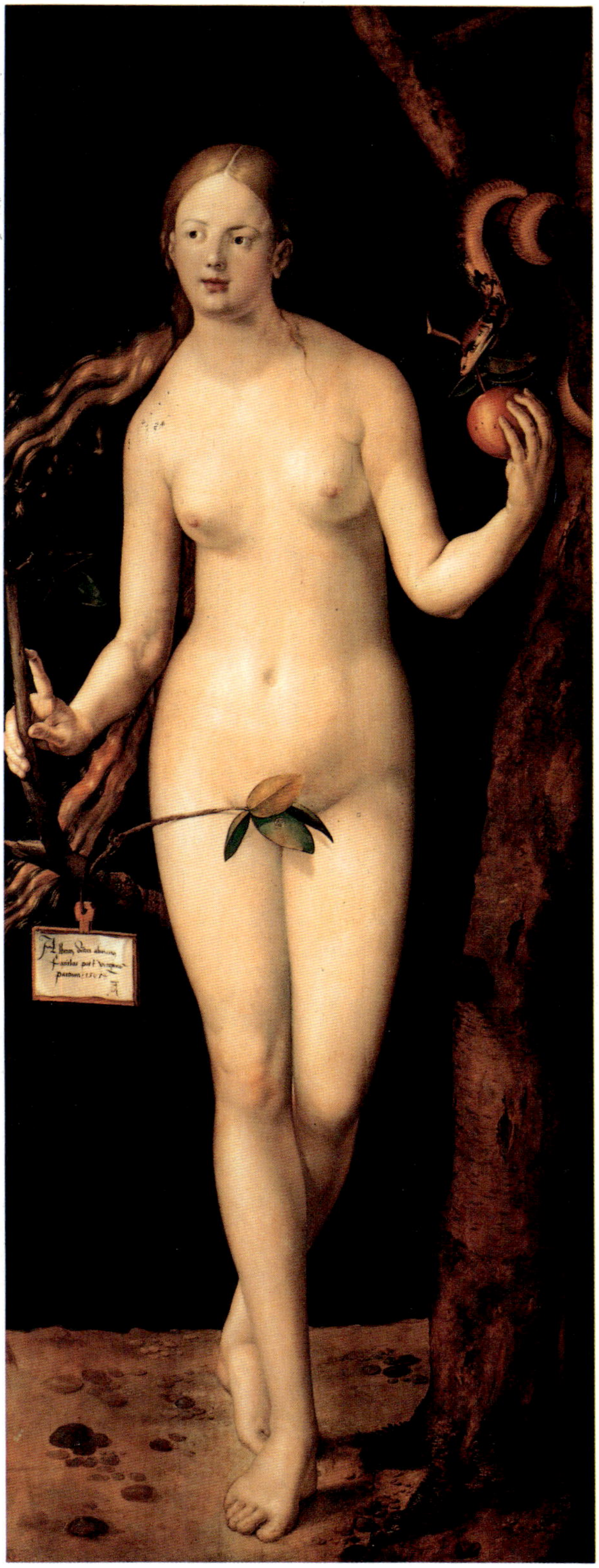

Eve

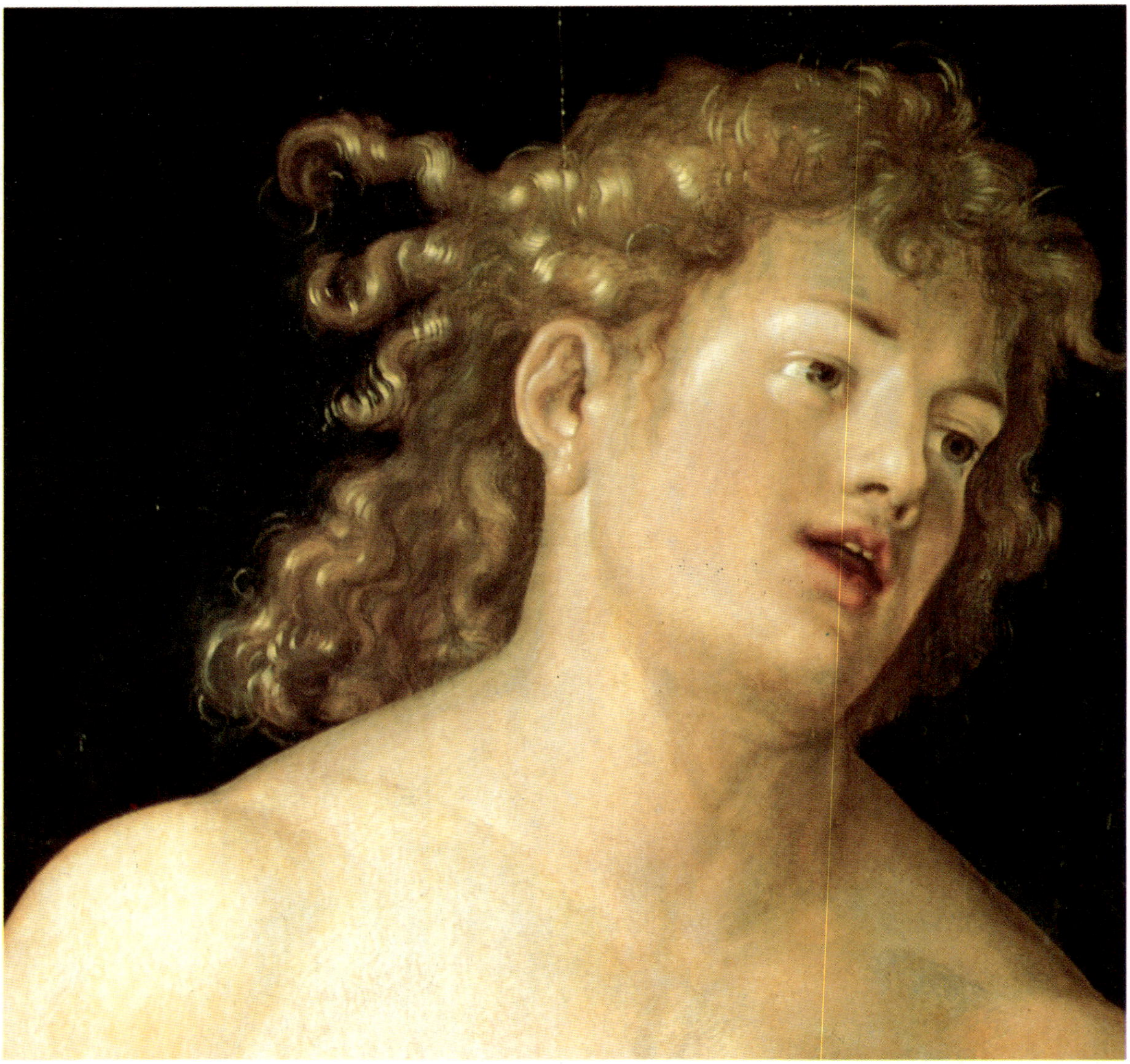

Adam (Detail)

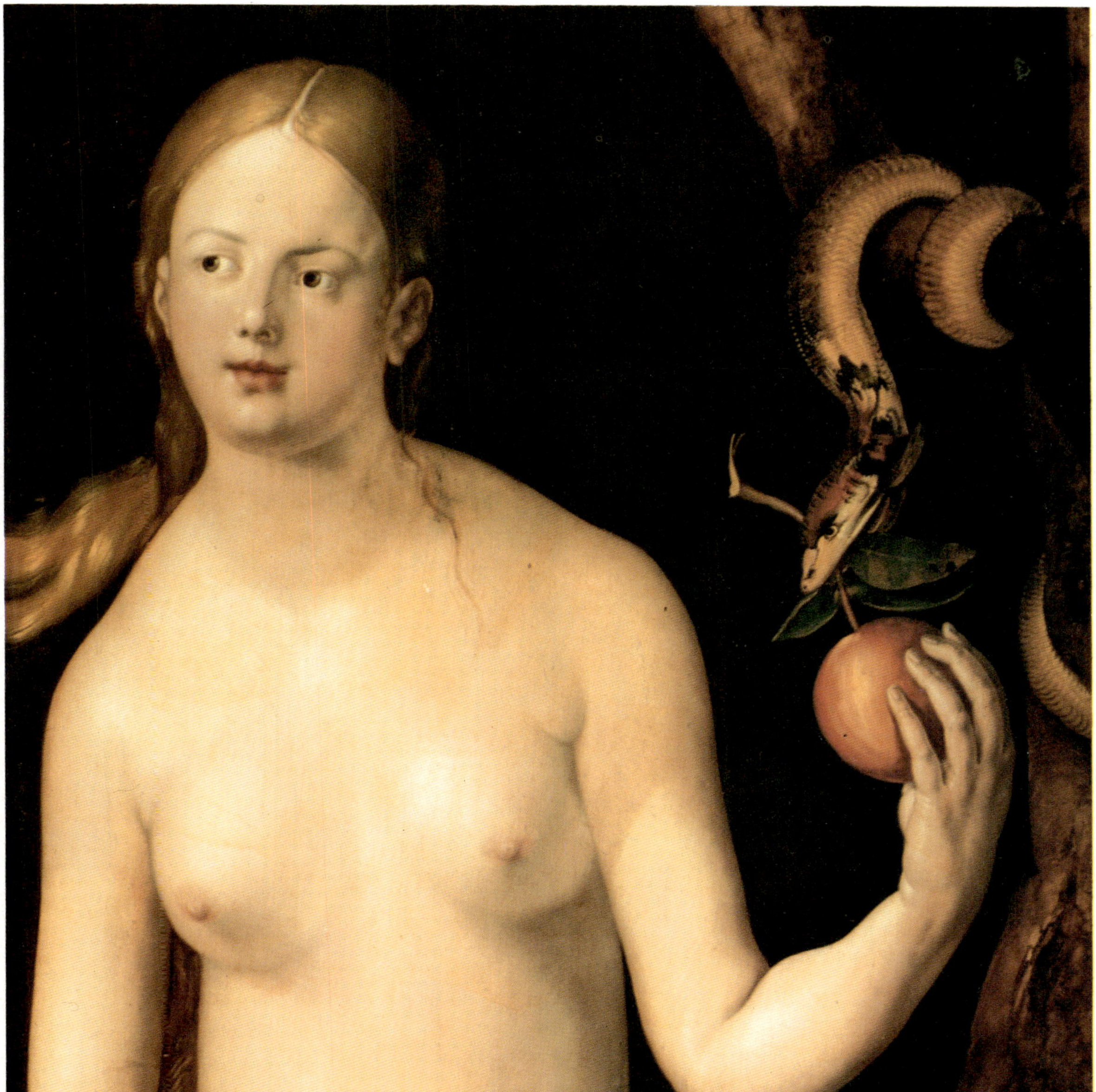

Eve (Detail)

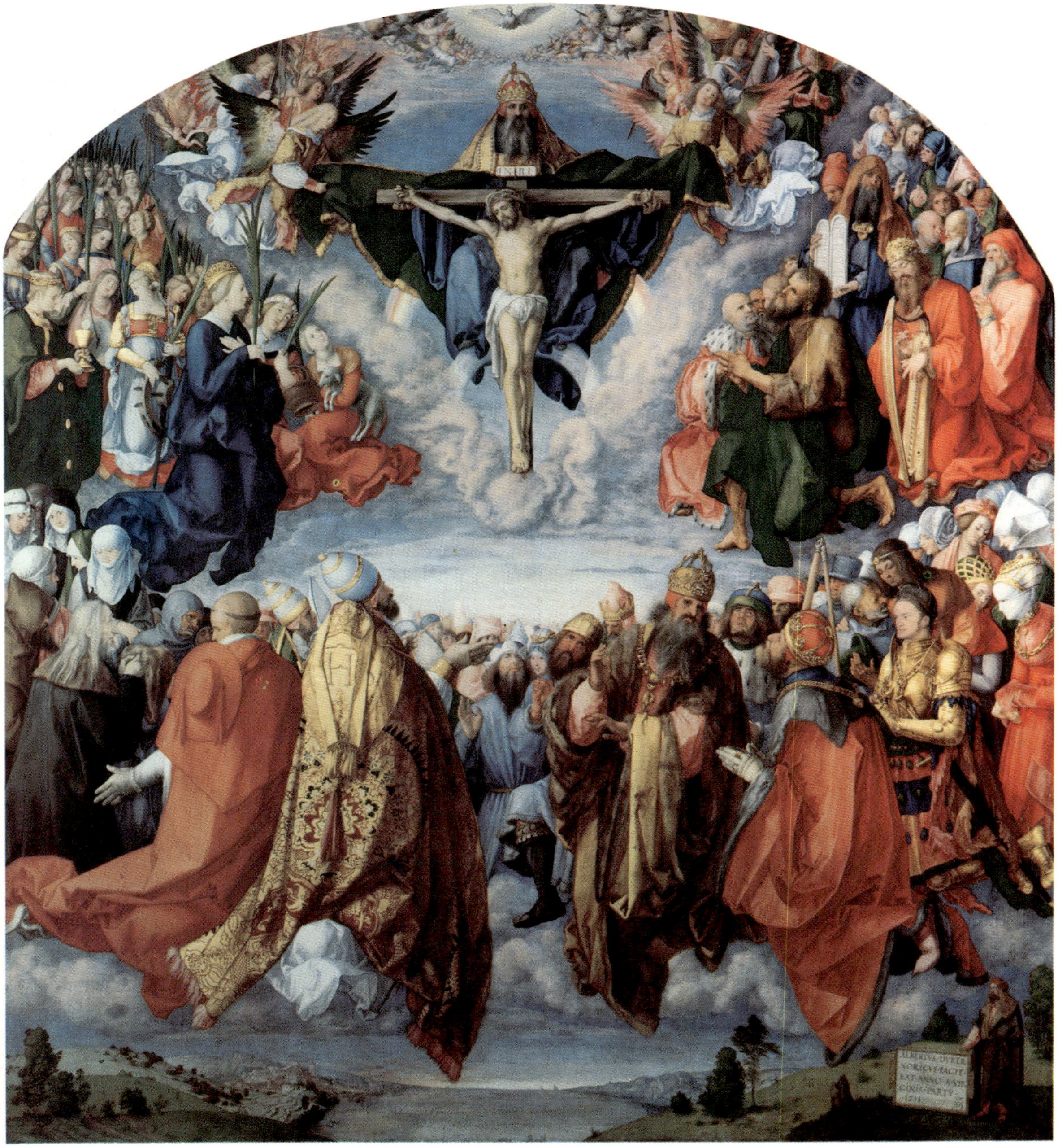

Adoration of the Trinity

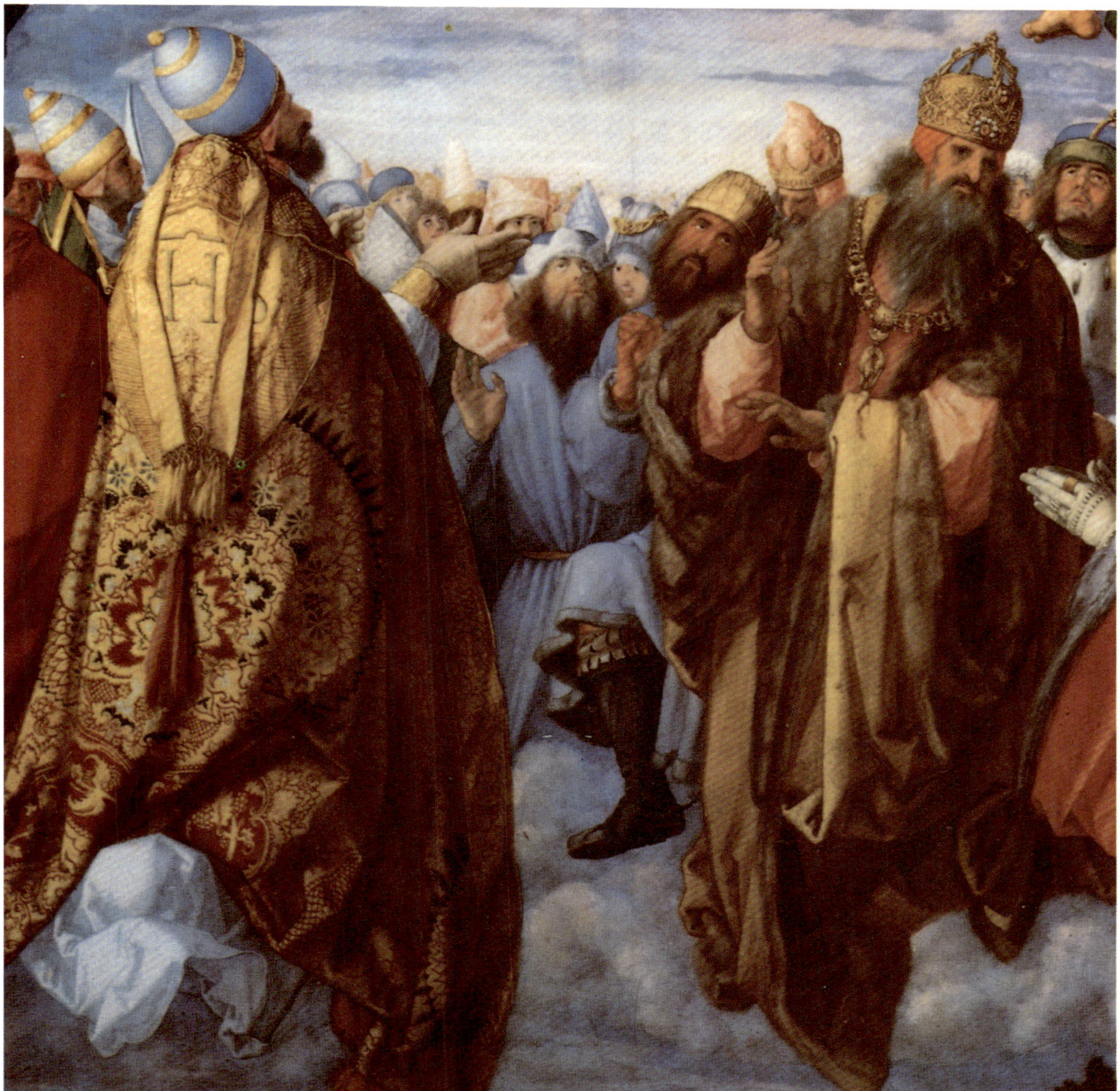

Adoration of the Trinity (Detail)

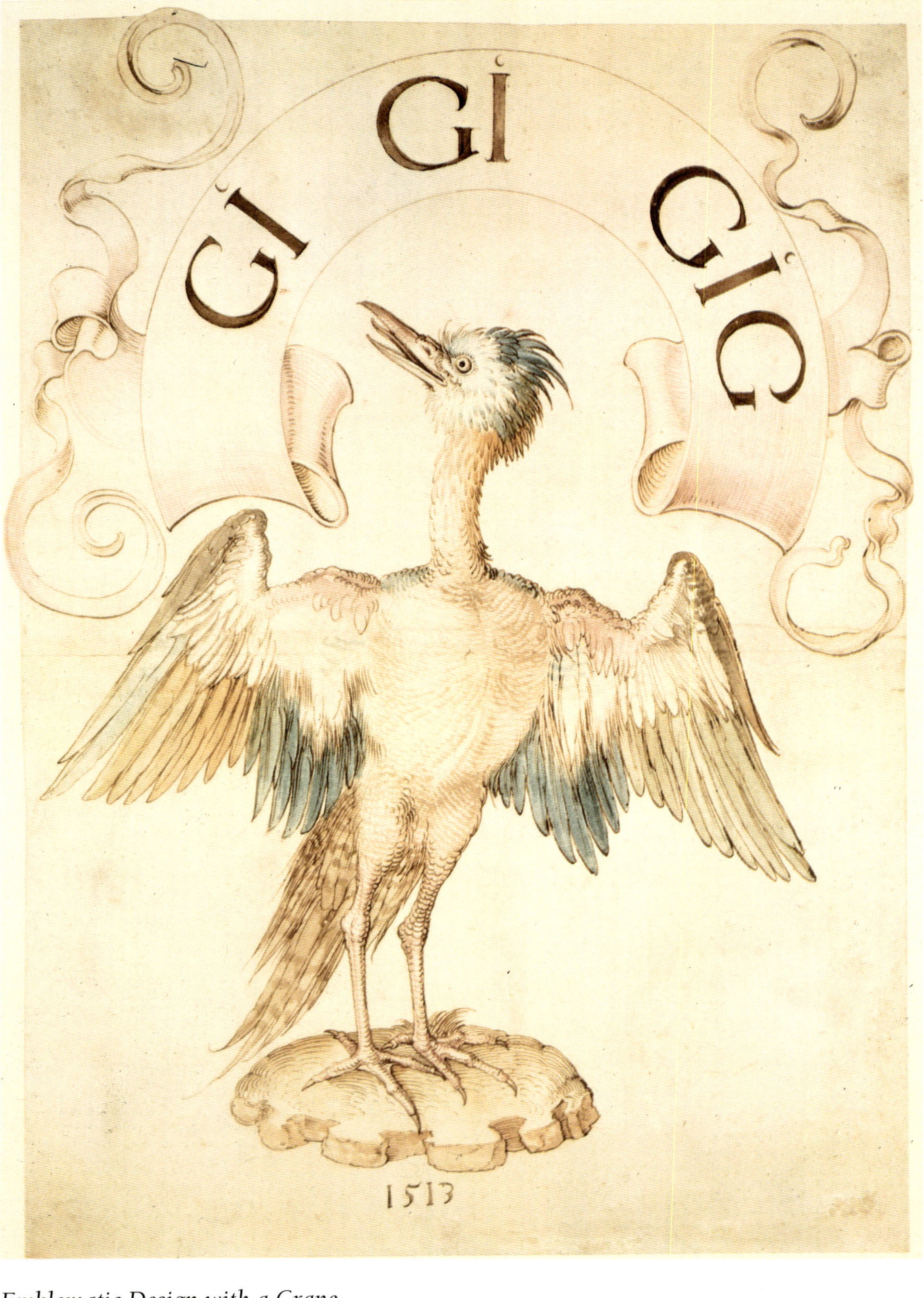

Emblematic Design with a Crane

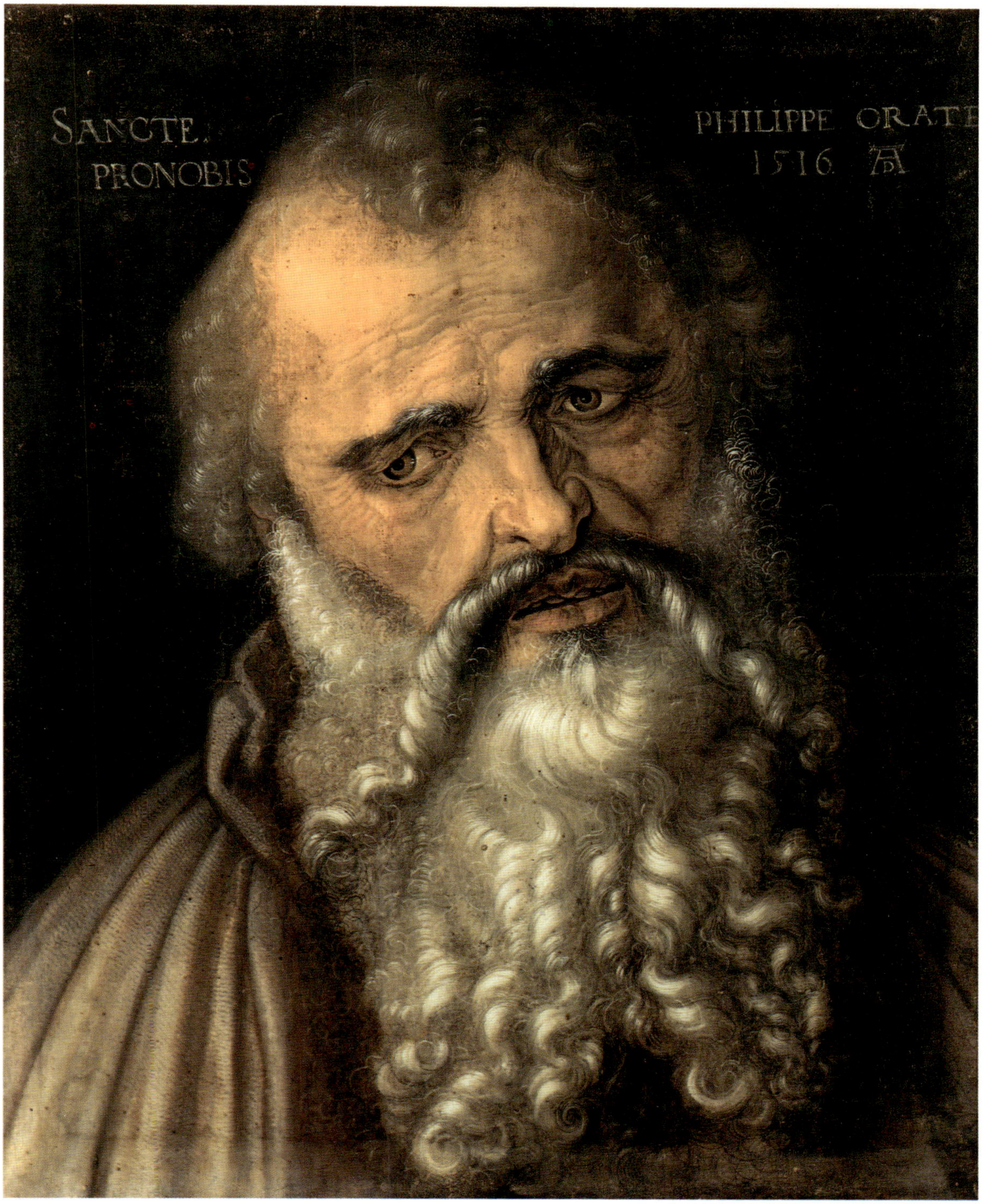

St Philip

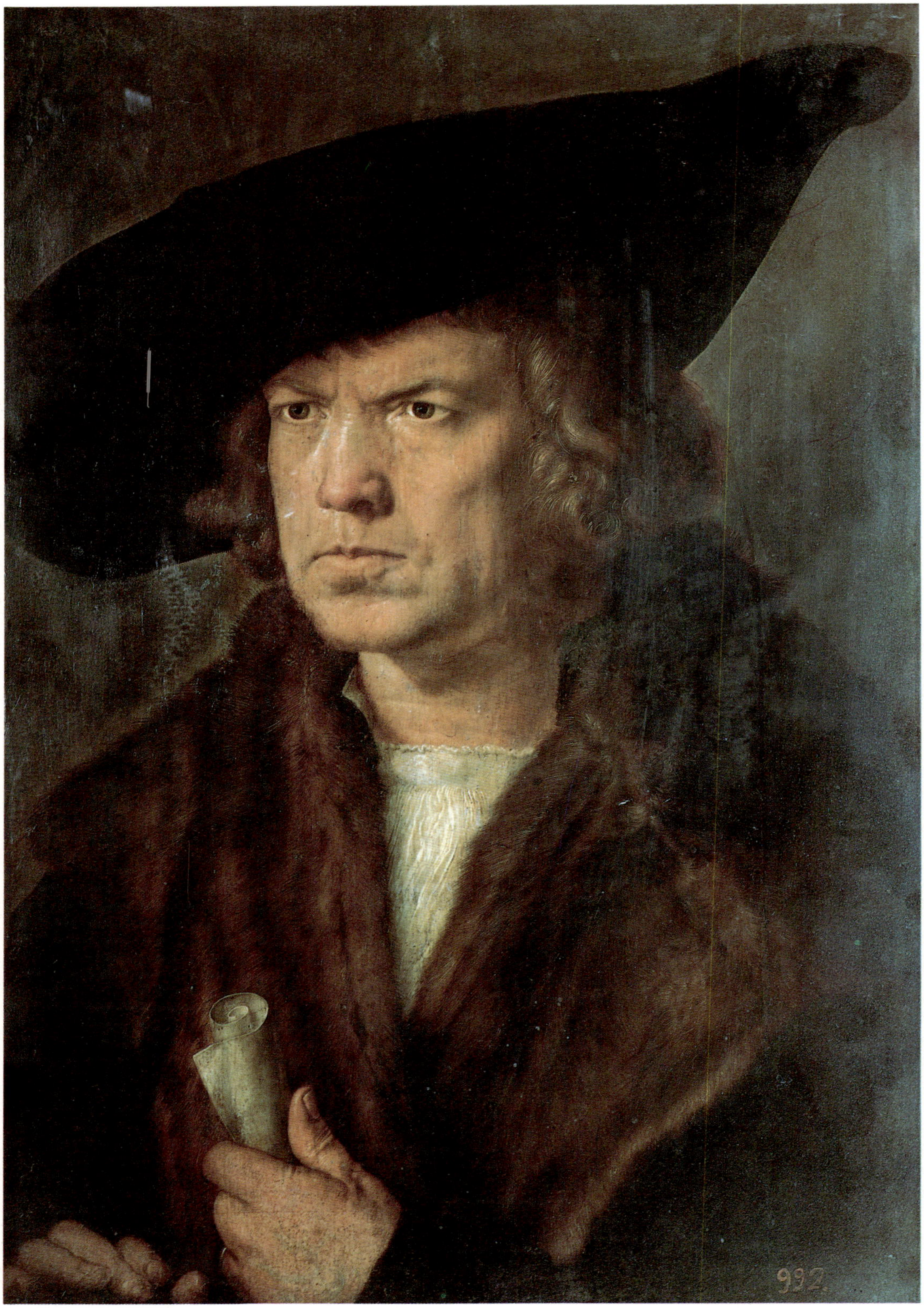

Portrait of a Gentleman

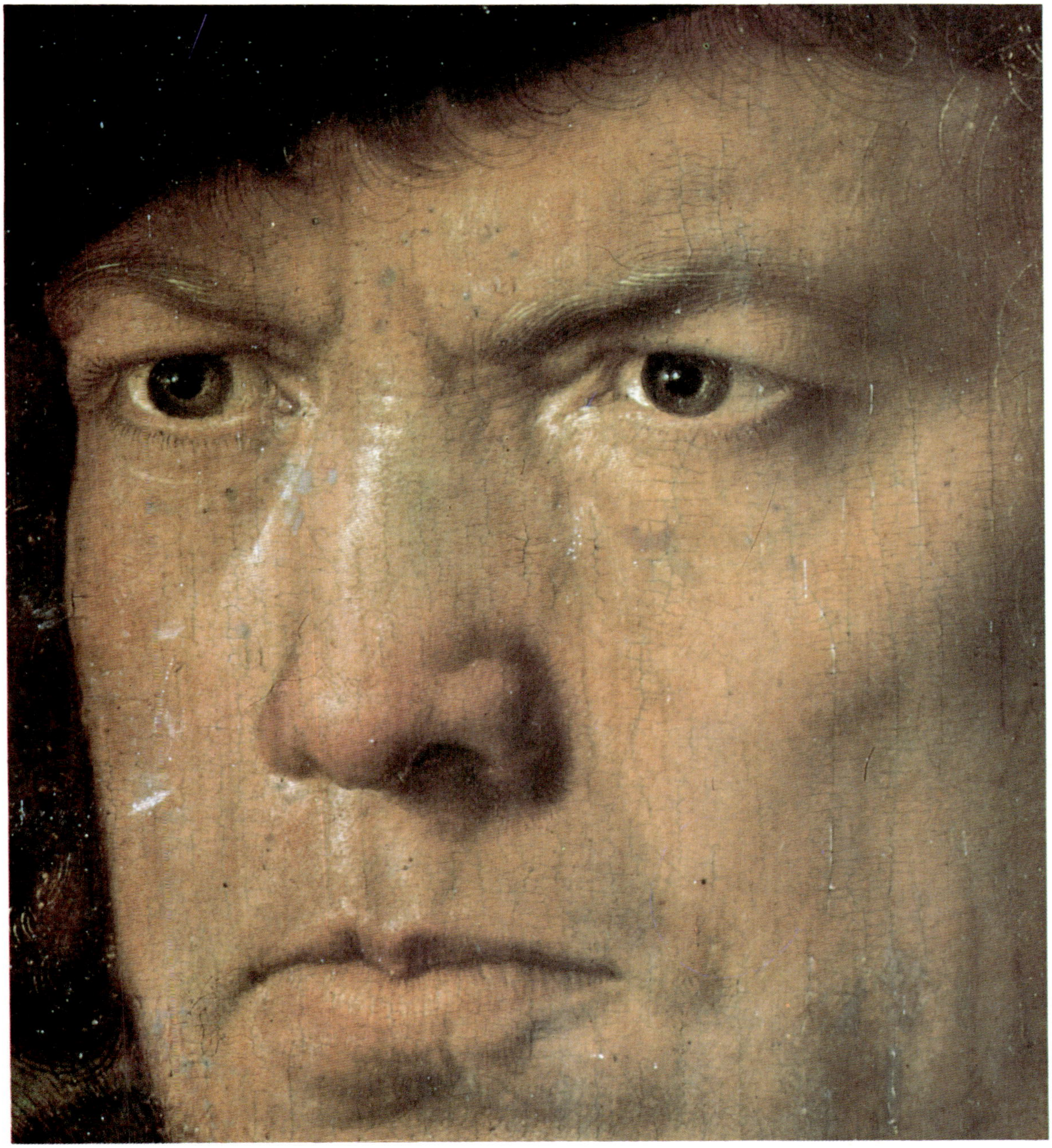

Portrait of a Gentleman (Detail)

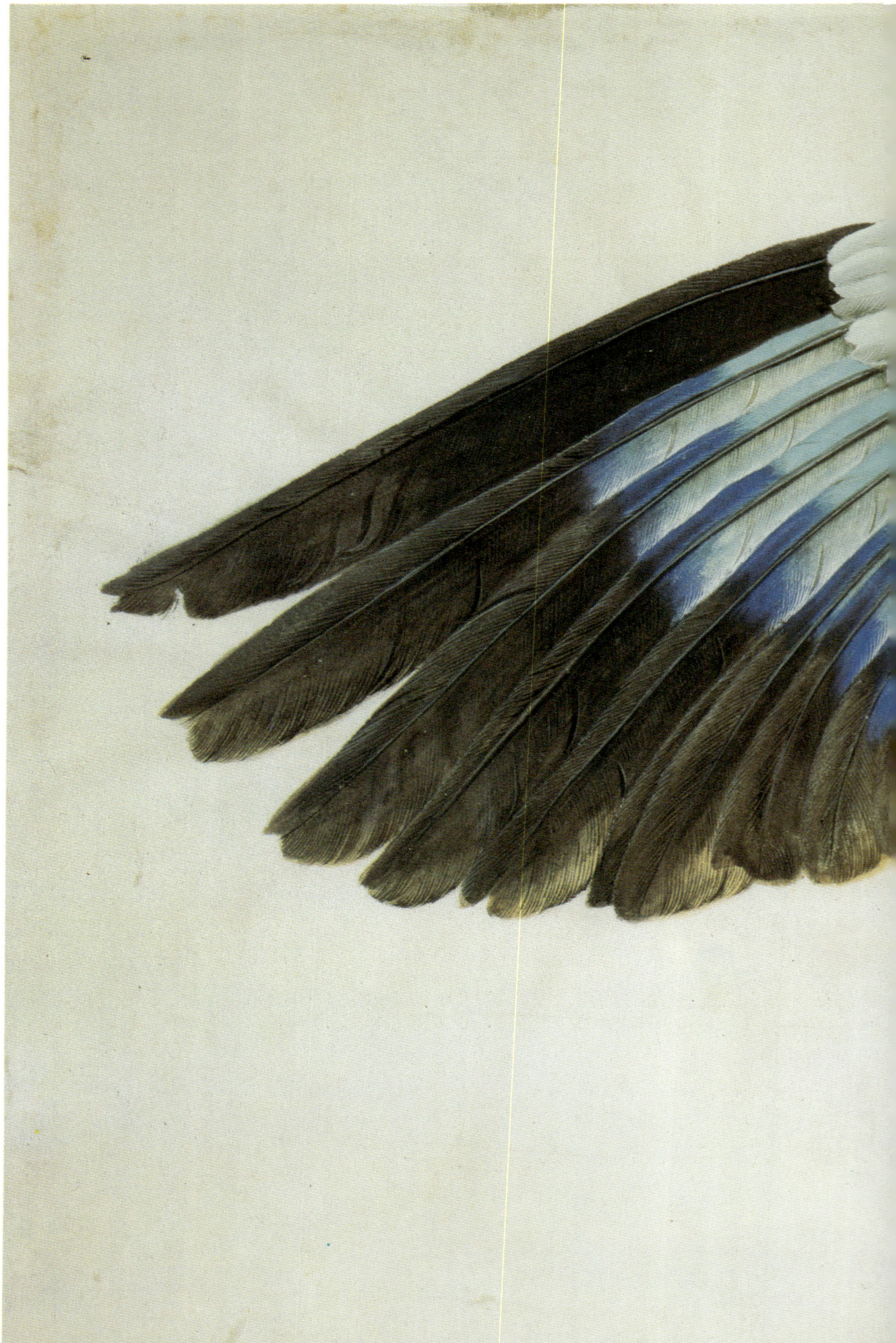

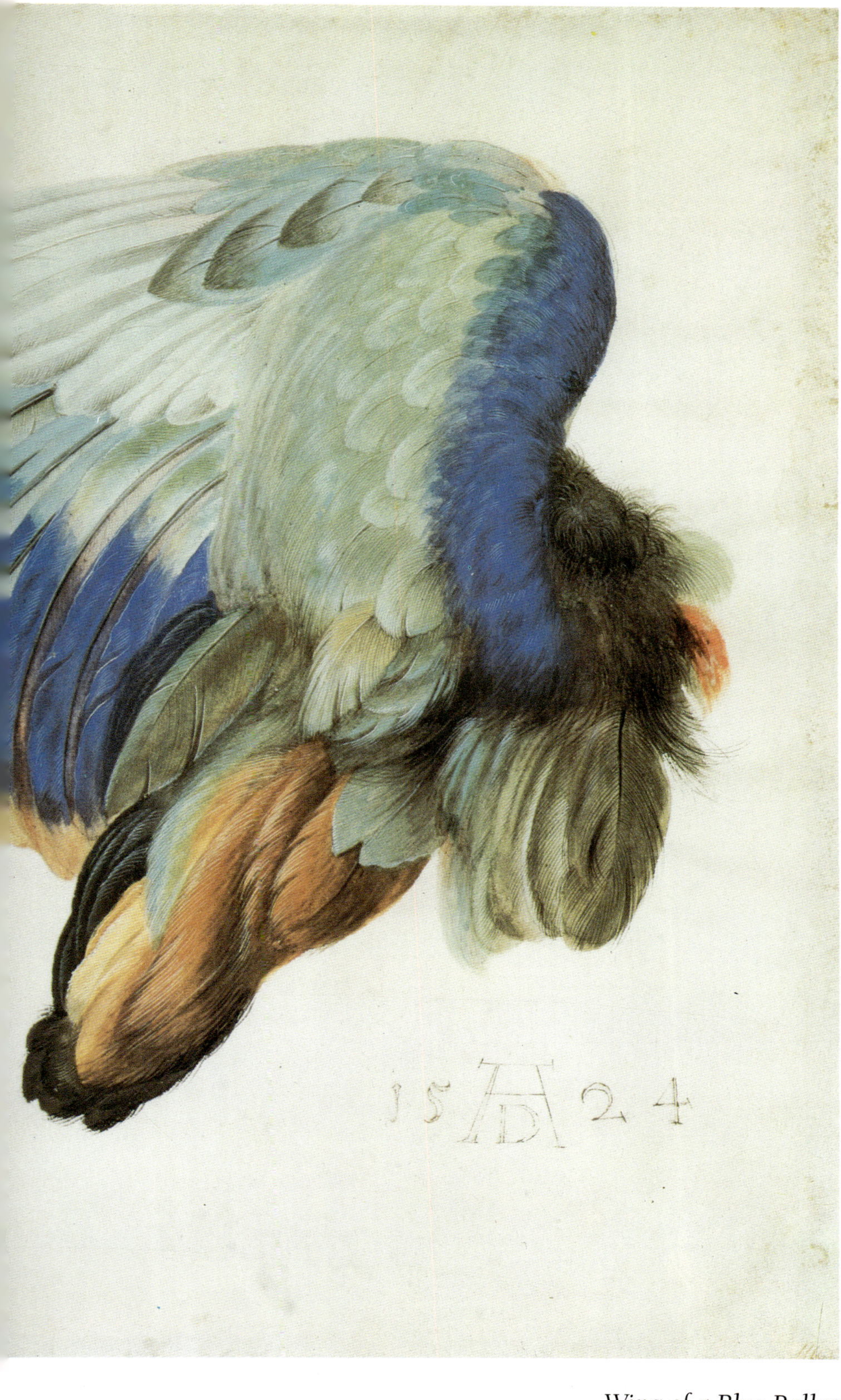

Wing of a Blue Roller

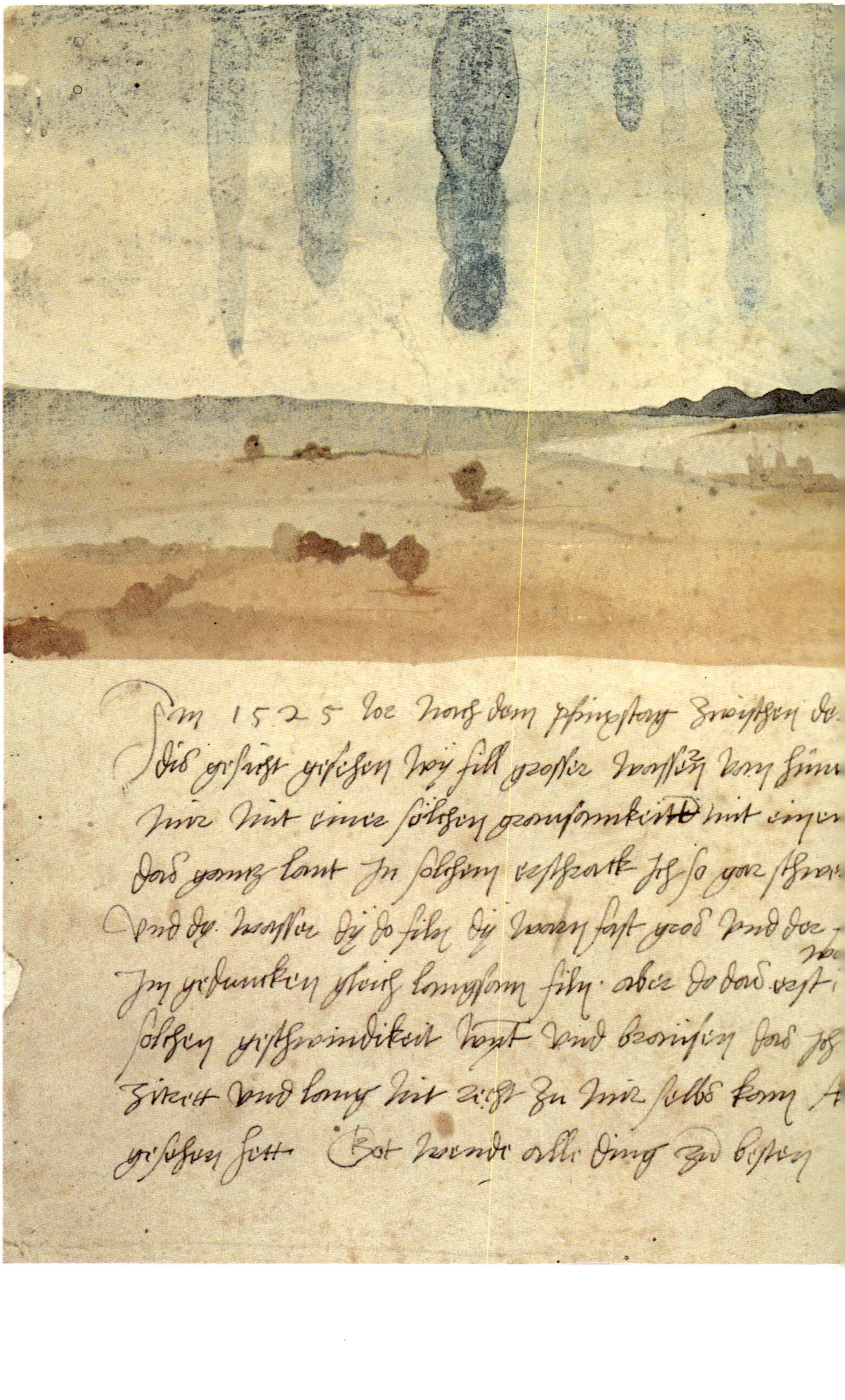
Im 1525 Jor noch dem pfingstag zwischen de
dis gesicht gesehen wy fill grosser wassern vom him
wir mit einer solchen grausamkeitt mit einer
das ganz lant Jn solchem erschrak Jch so gar sehr
Und do dy wasser dy do filn dy waren fast groß und der
Jn gedancken gleich langsam filn aber do das erst
solchen geschwindikeit wint und brausen das Jch
zitert und lang nit zw mir selbs kam A
gesehen hett Got wende alle ding zu besten

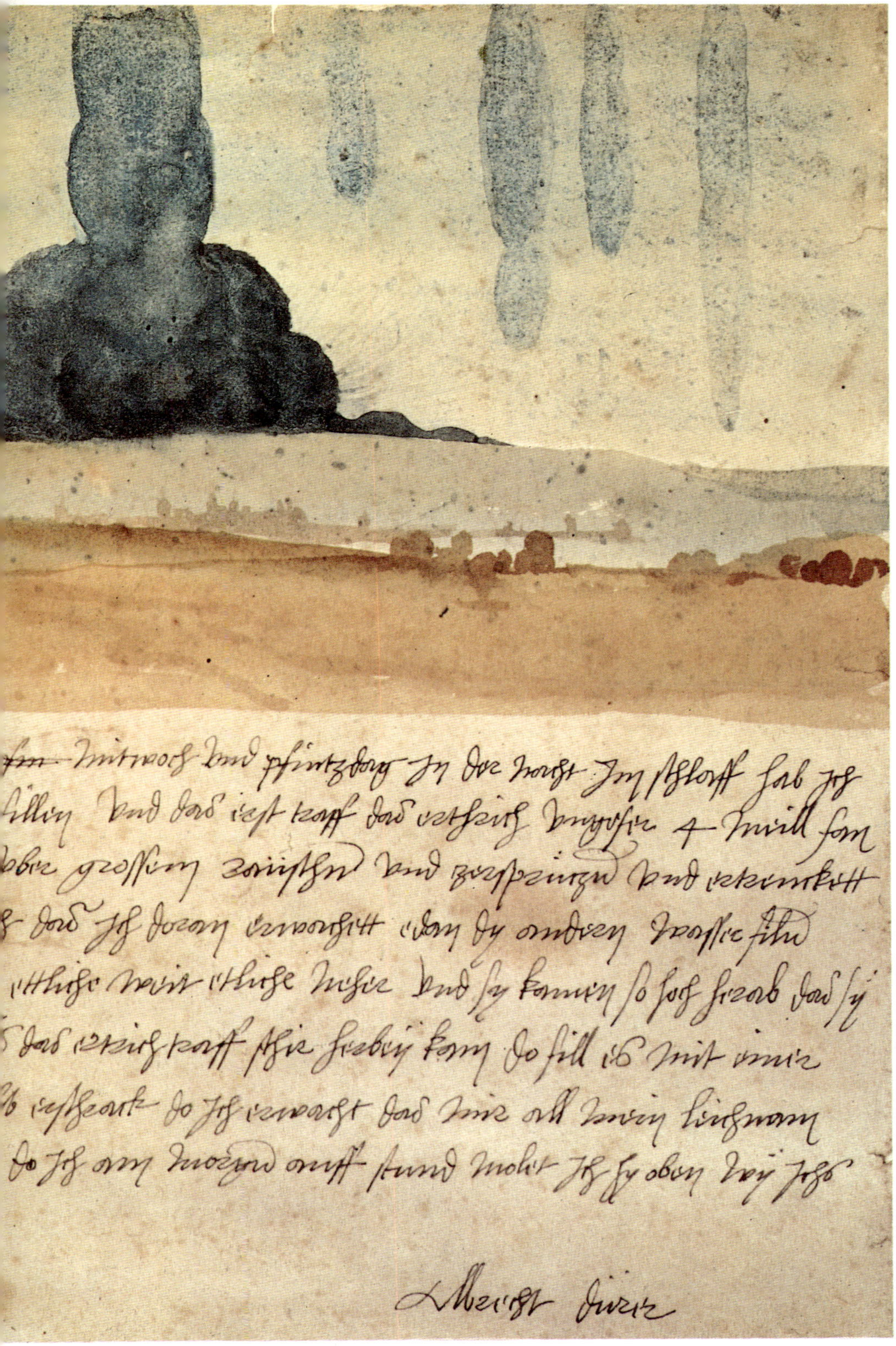

Flood (Dream Vision)

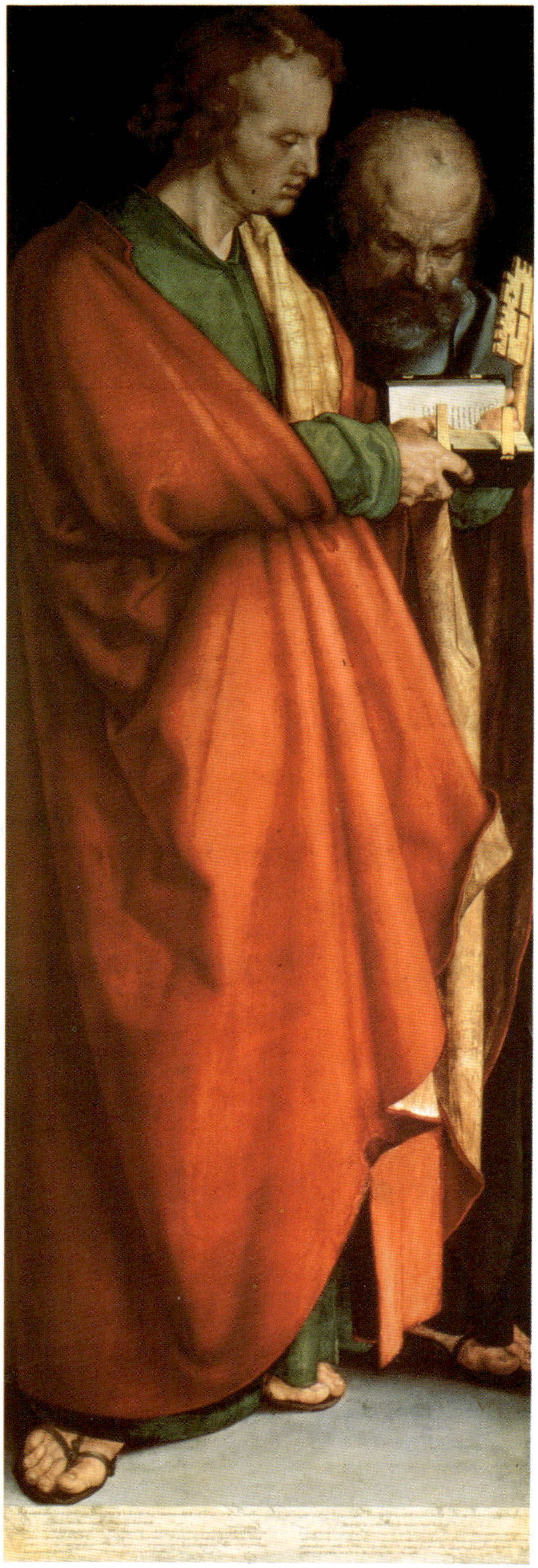

The Four Apostles (Detail) *St John and St Peter*

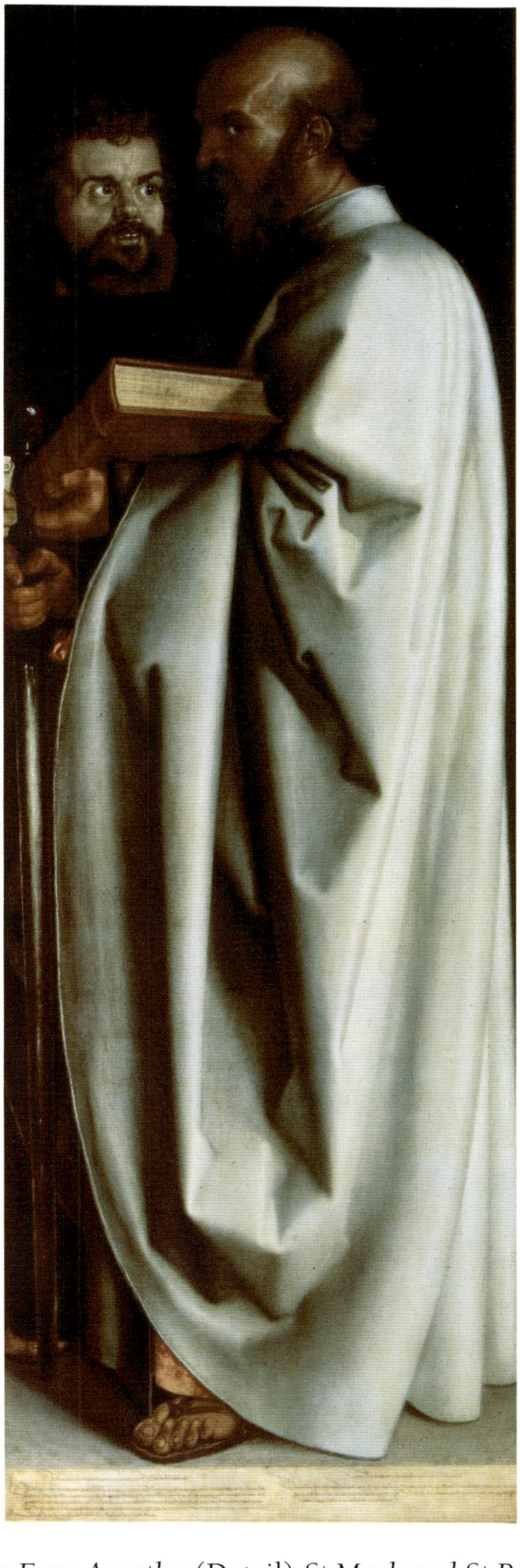

The Four Apostles (Detail) *St Mark and St Paul*

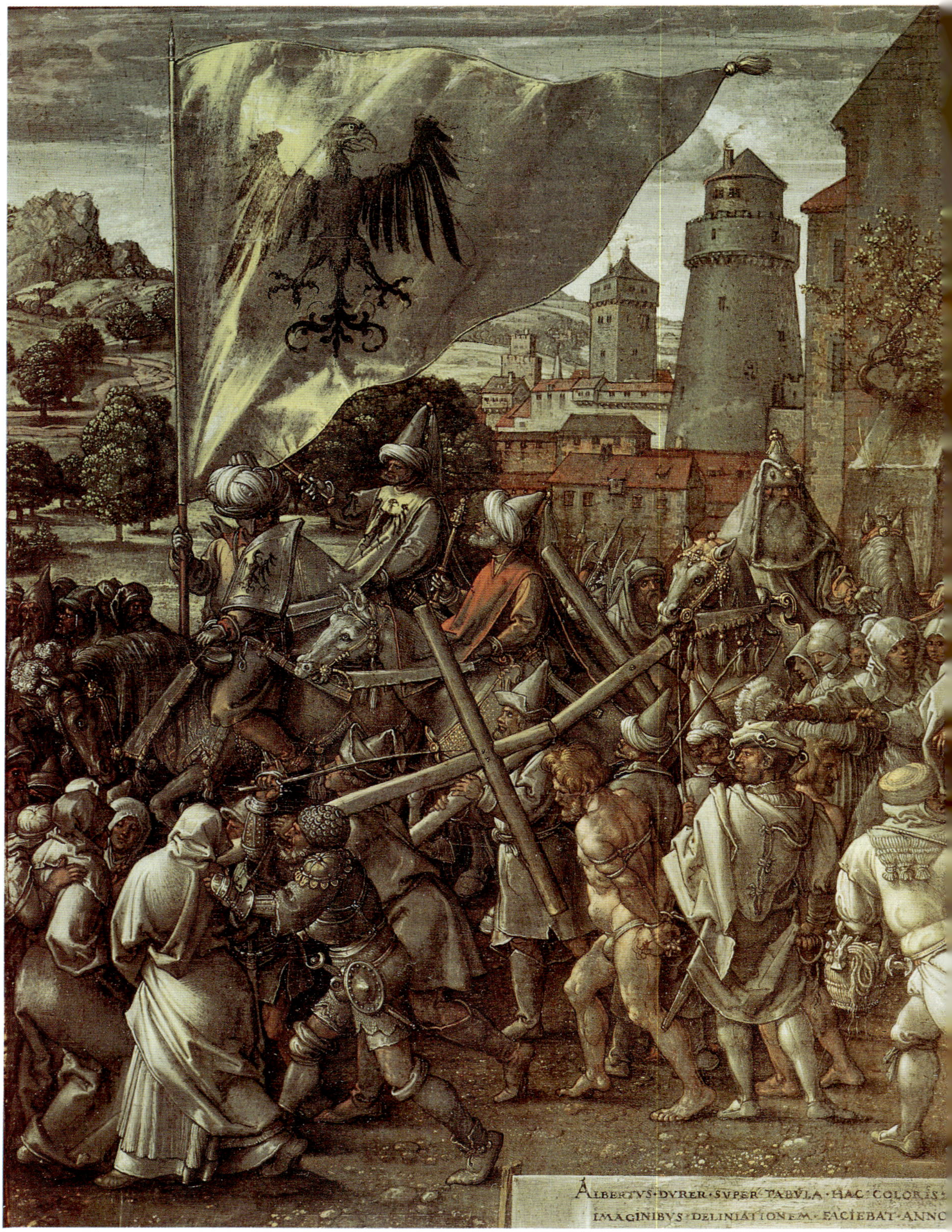
ALBERTVS·DVRER·SVPER TABVLA·HAC COLORIS
IMAGINIBVS·DELINIATIONEM·FACIEBAT·ANNO

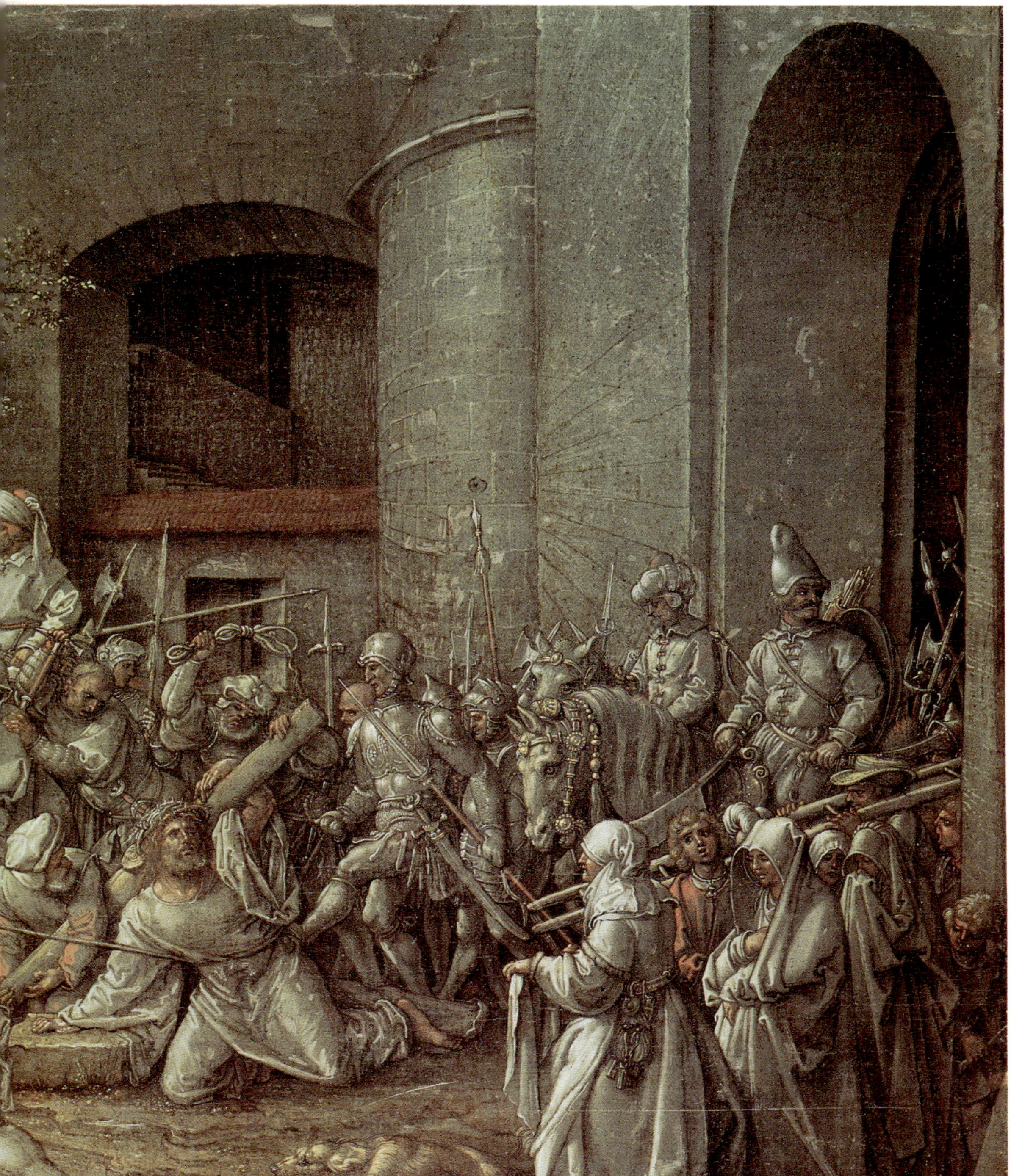

Bearing of the Cross

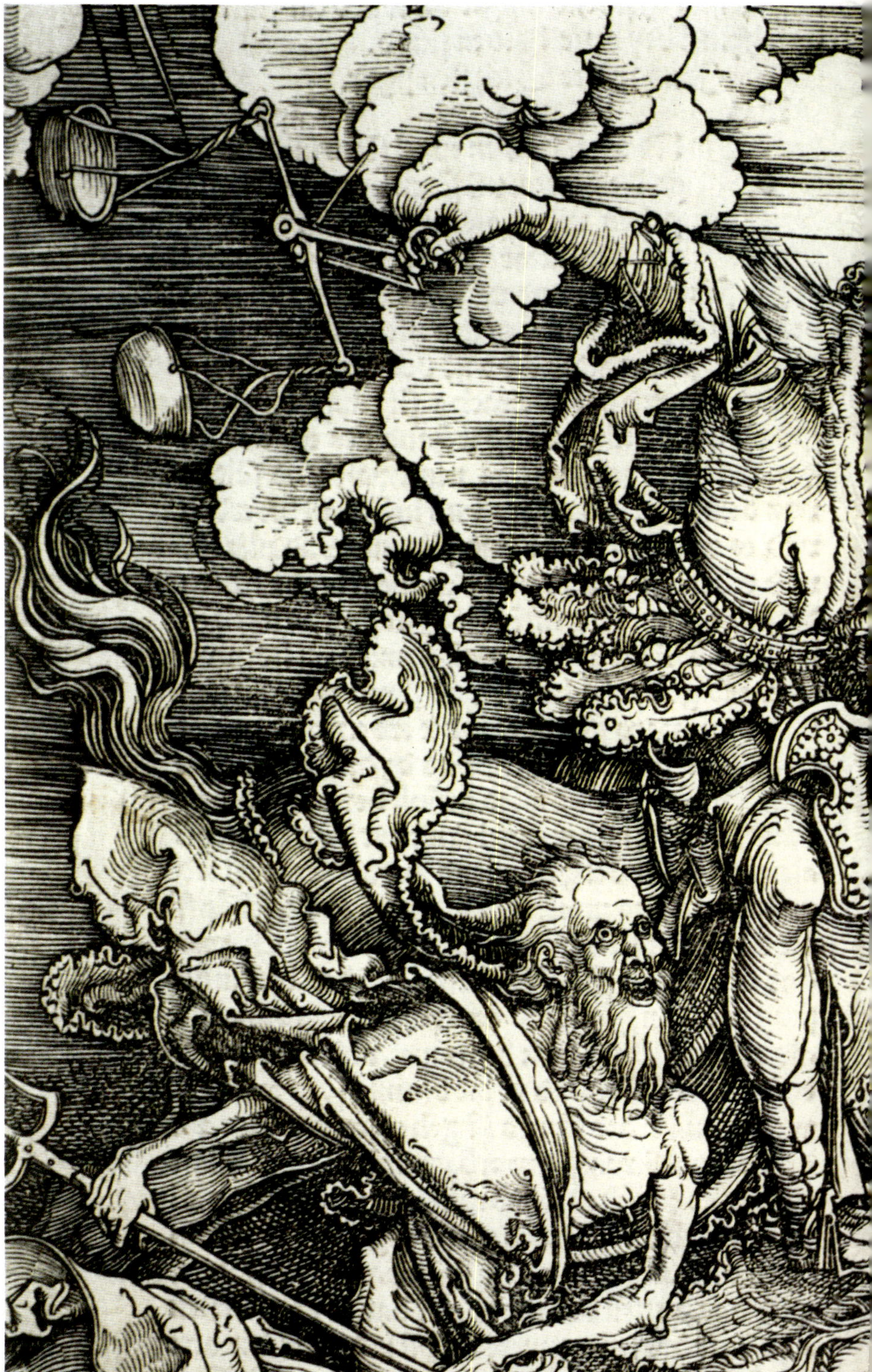

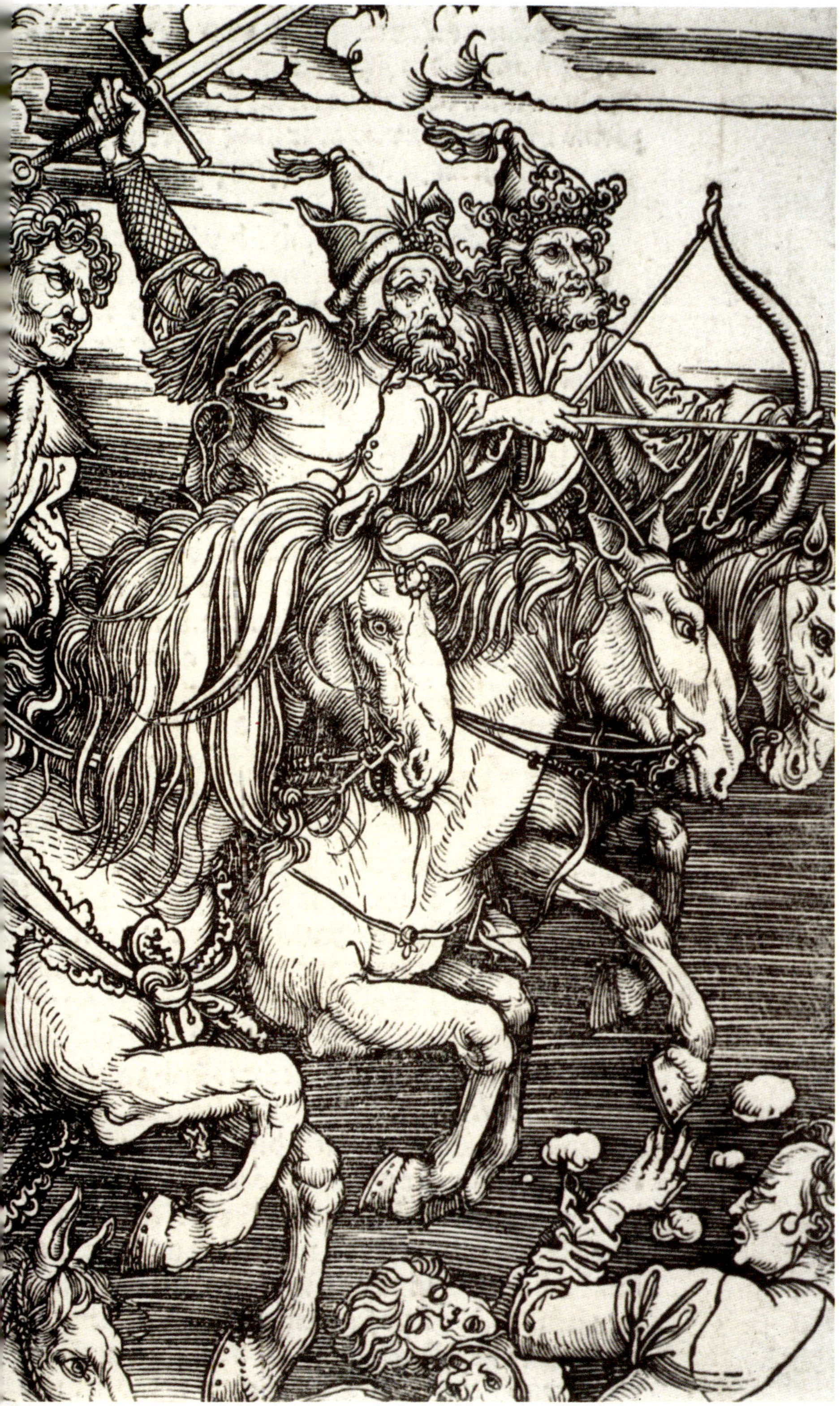

The Four Horsemen of the Apocalypse

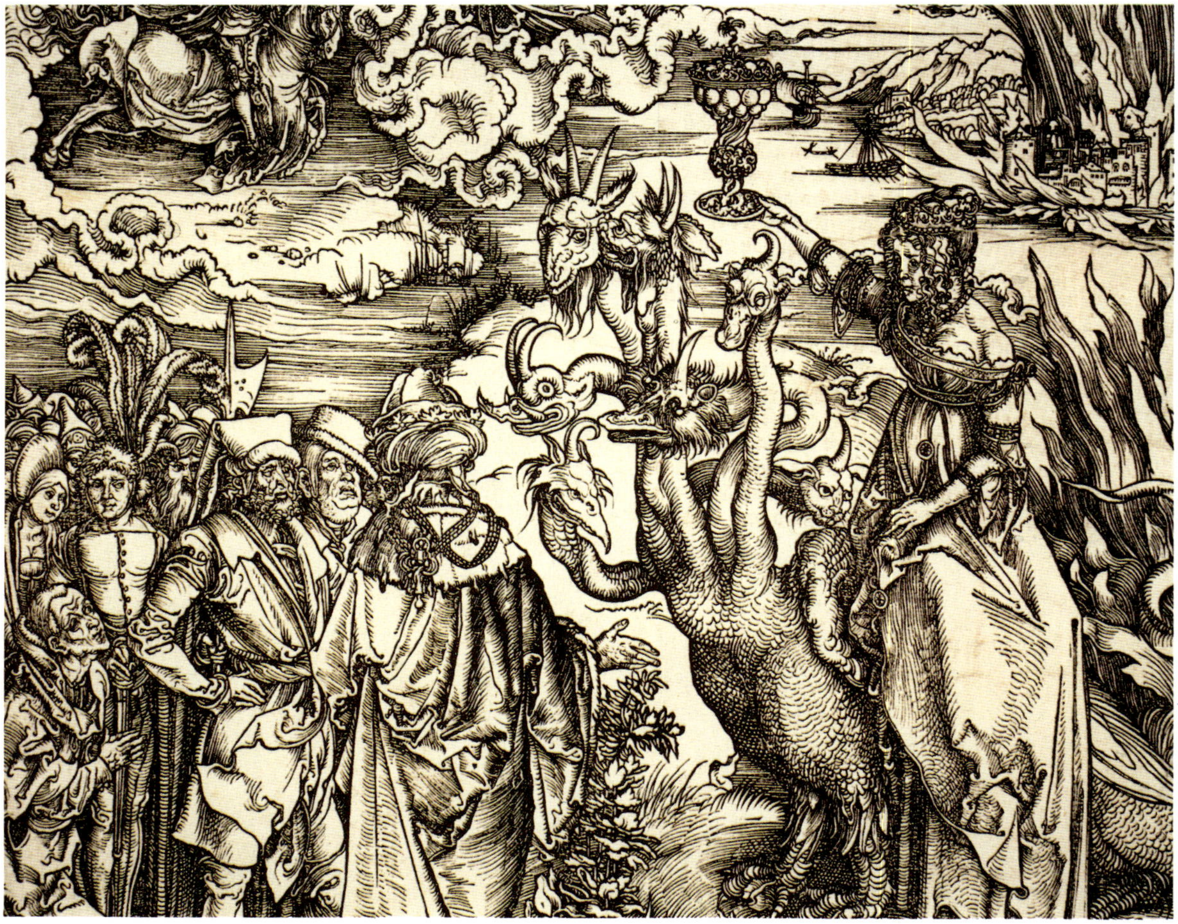

The Apocalypse (Detail)

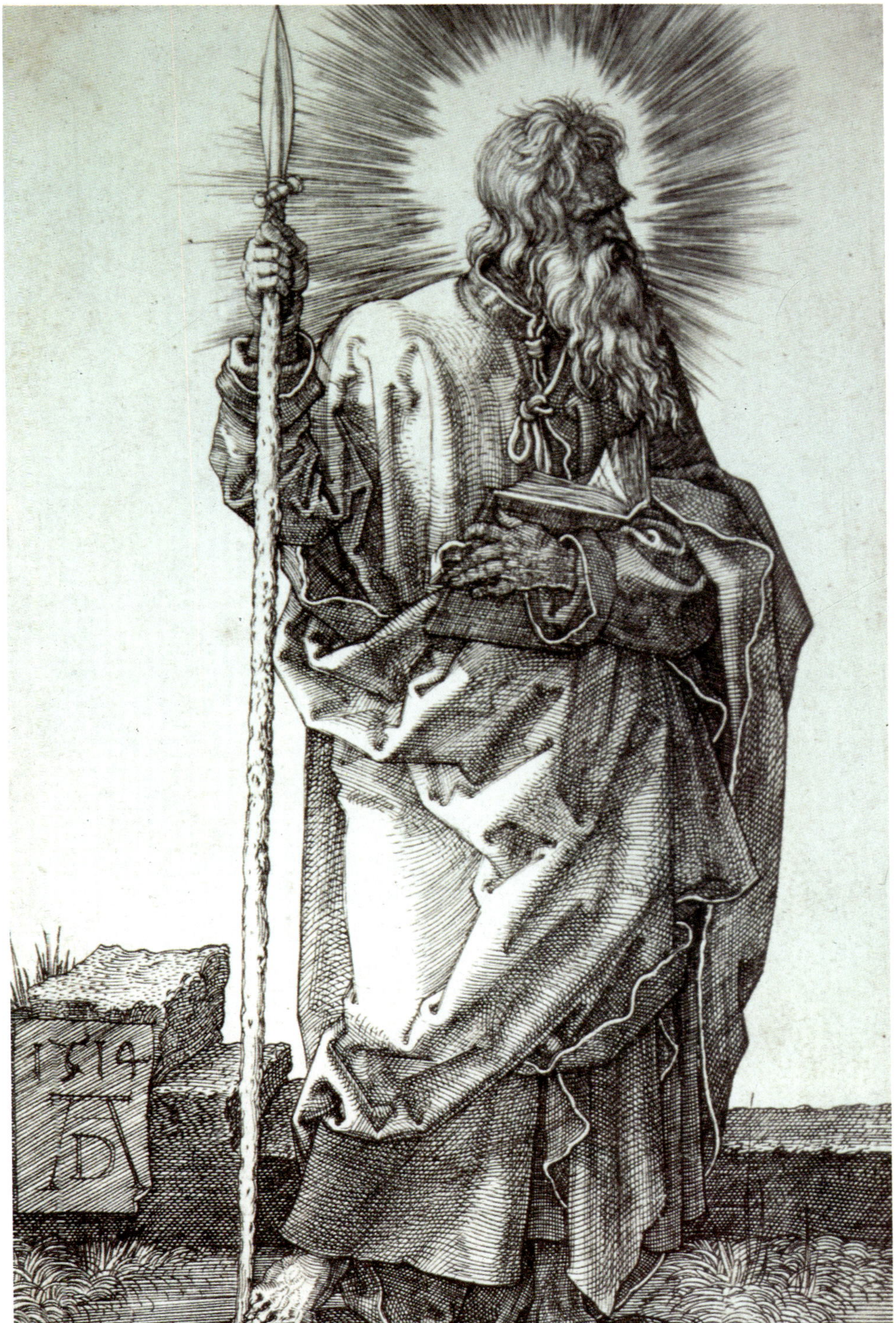

Apostle

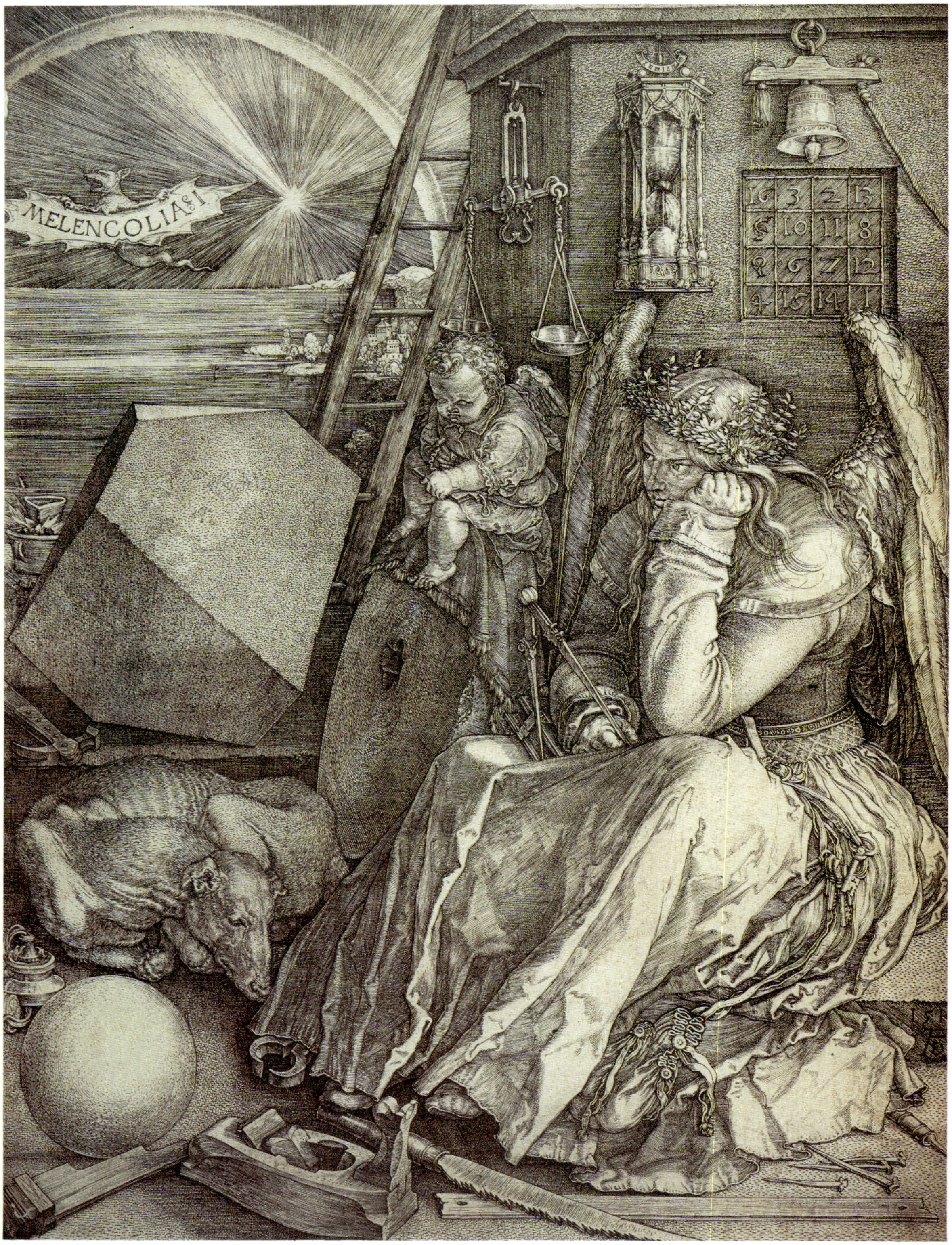

Melancholy I

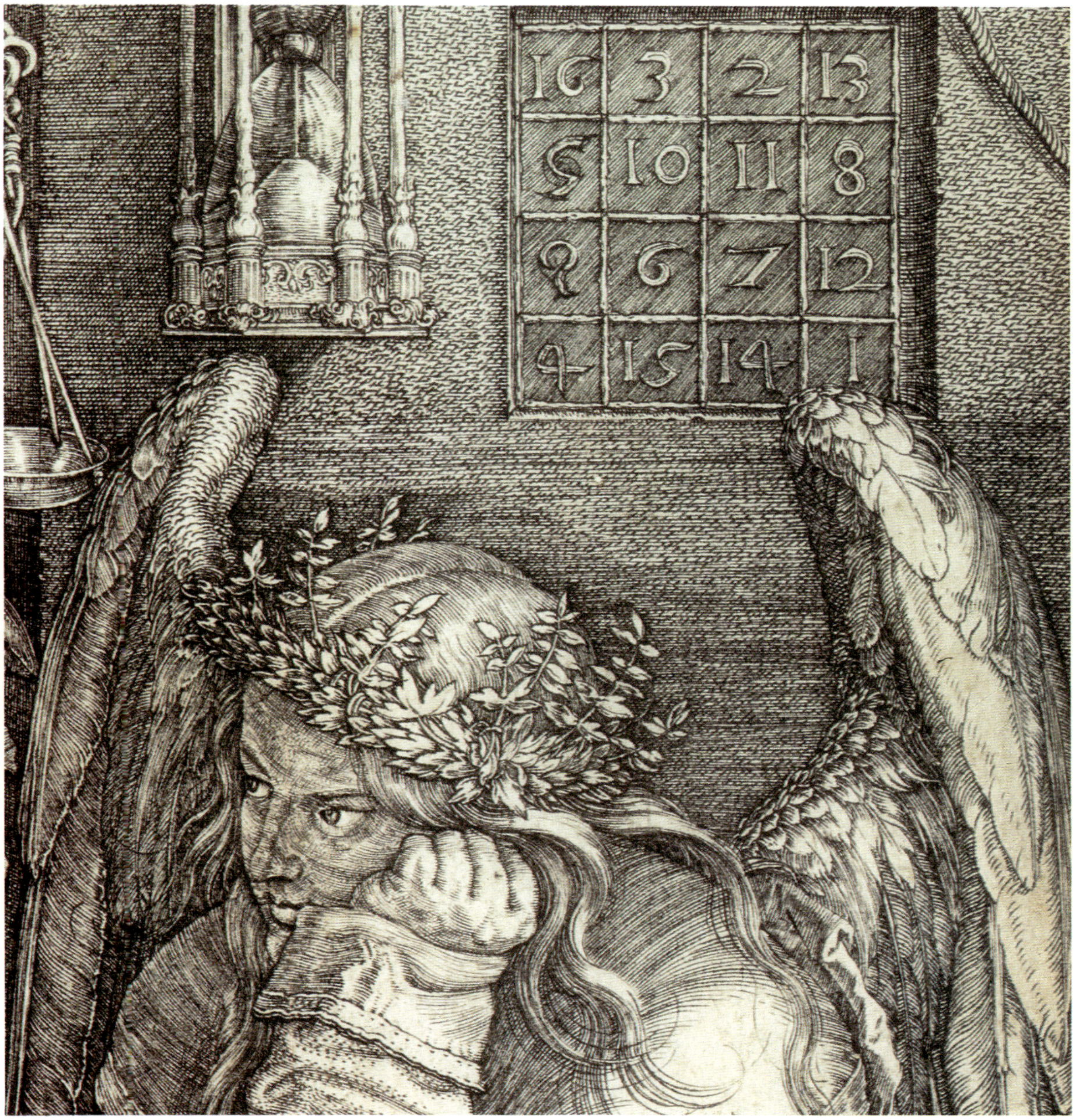

Melancholy I (Detail)

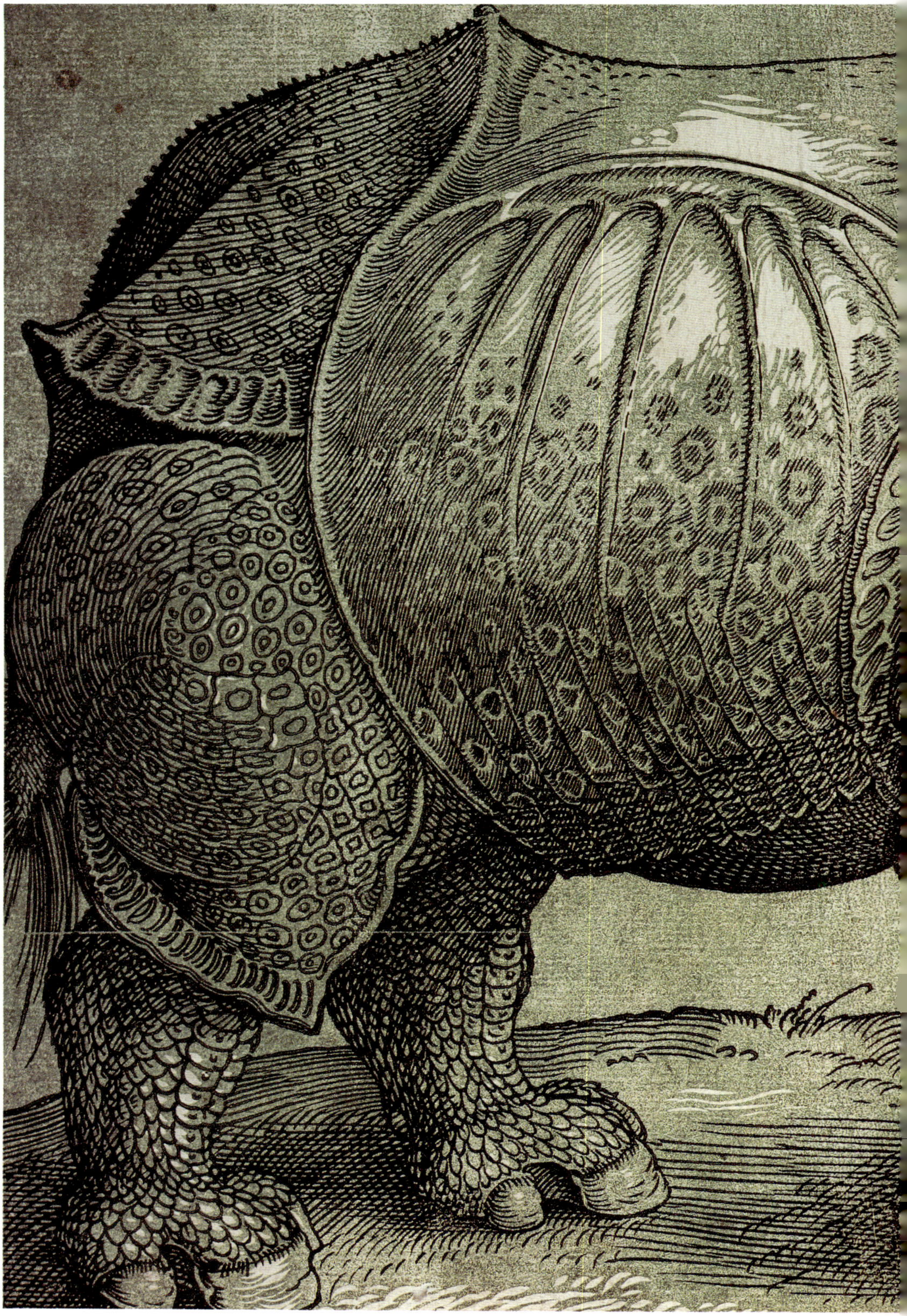

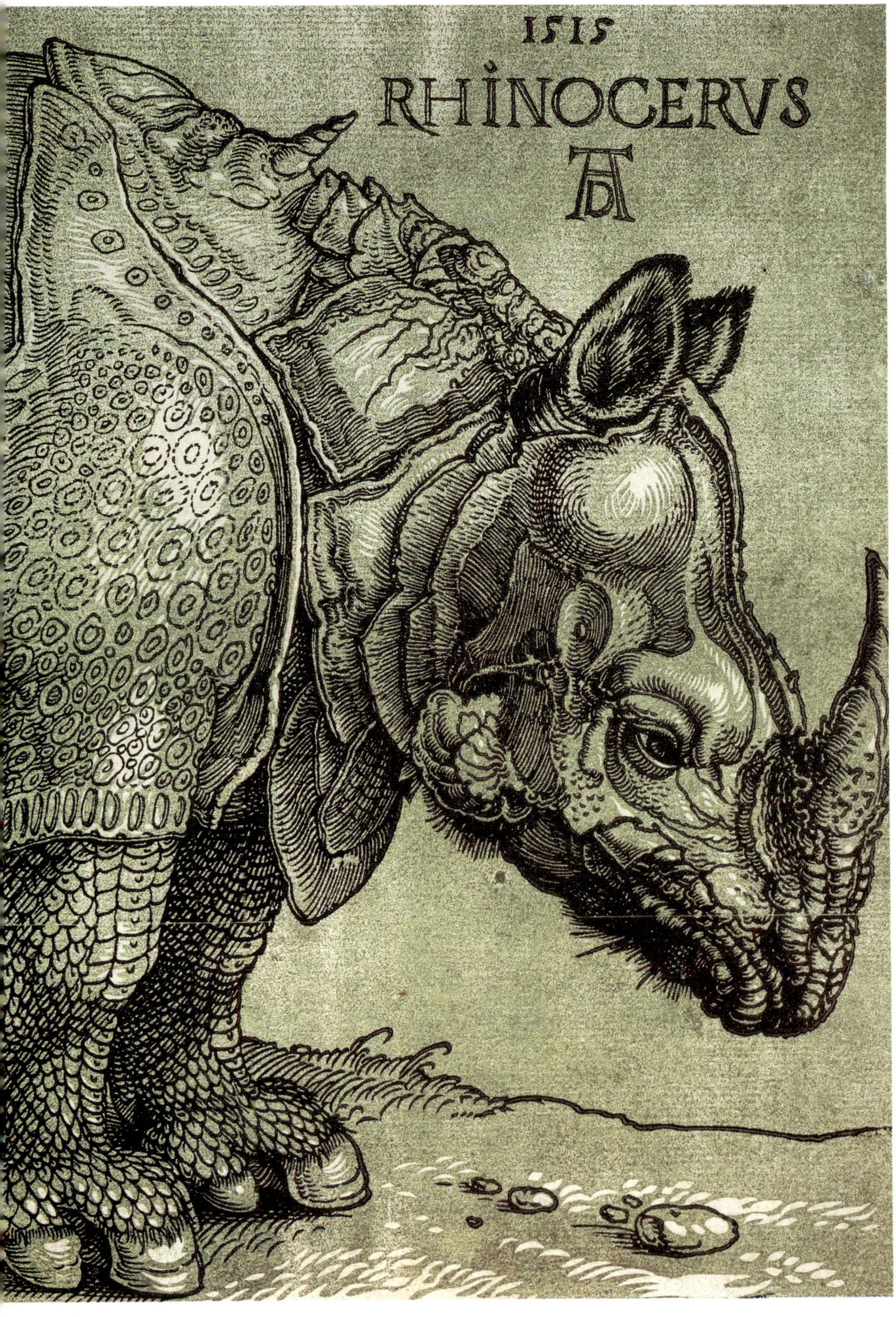

The Rhinoceros

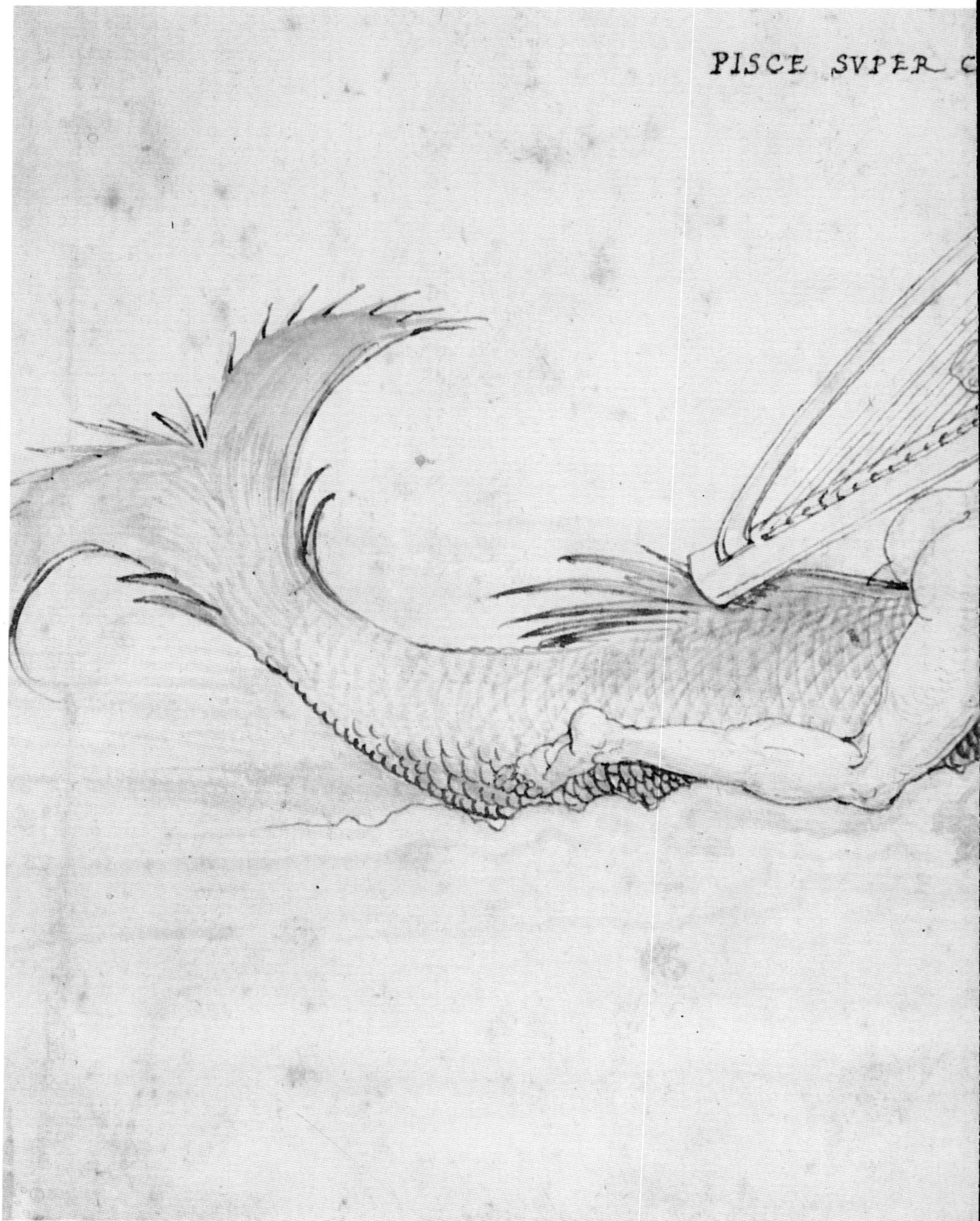
PISCE SVPER C

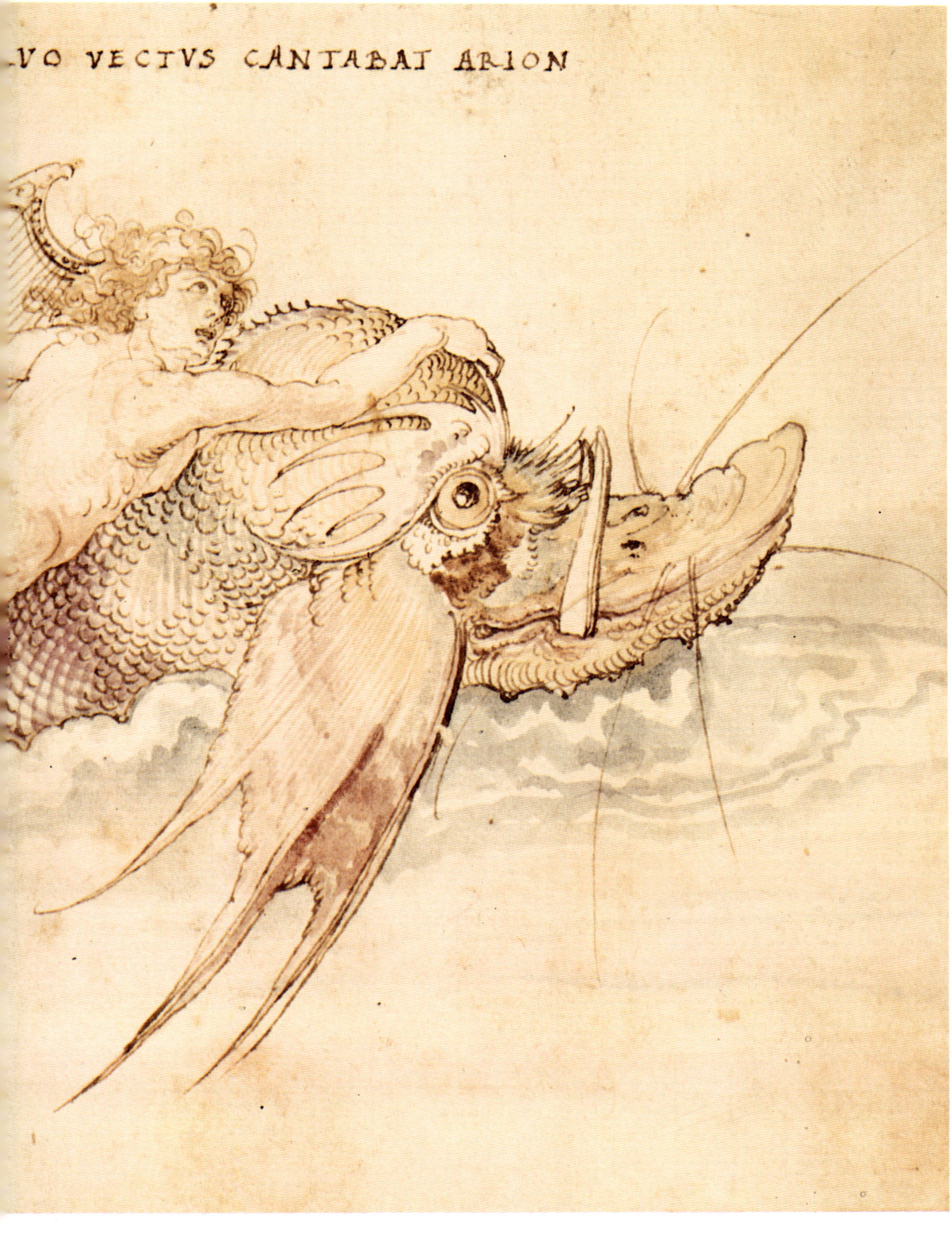

Arion

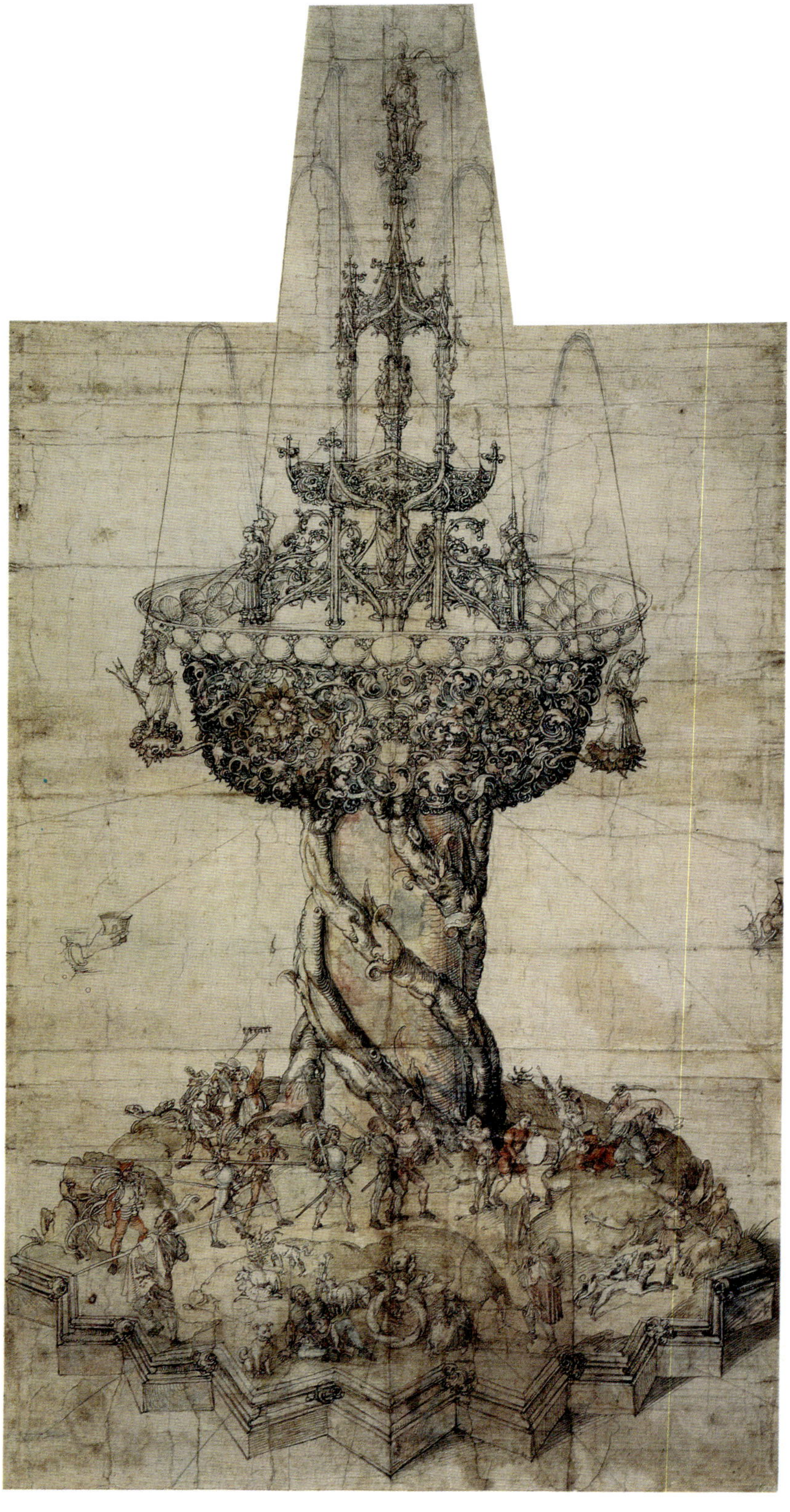

Fountain

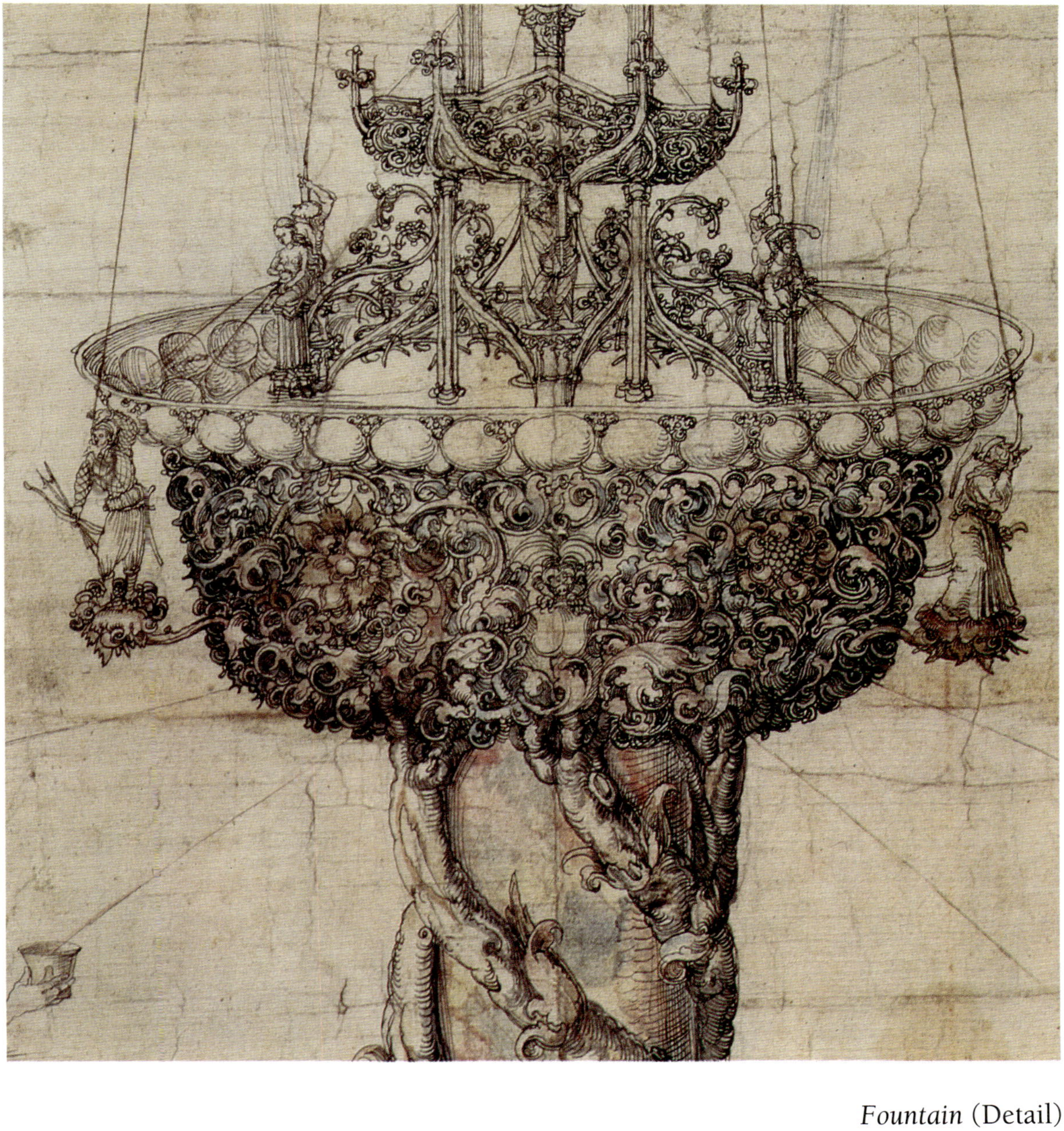

Fountain (Detail)

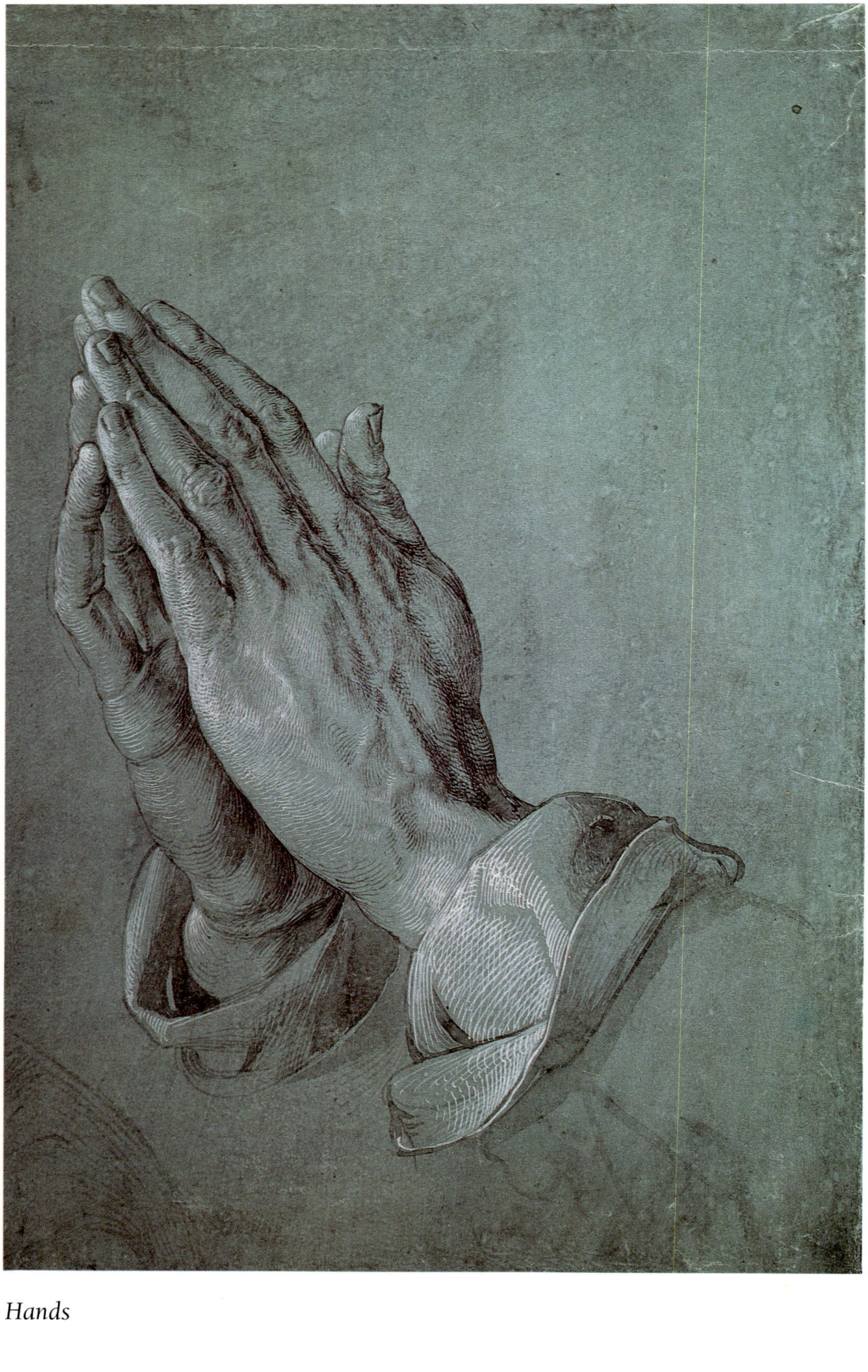

Hands

Stampa Grafiche Editoriali Padane Cremona